Middle School Pathfinders:

Guiding Student Research

by Nancy J. Keane

LINWORTH
LEARNING

Activities & Resources
From the Minds of Teachers

To my children, Aureta and Alex Keane
and my new grandsons, Aiden and Jordan.
And to the memory of my mother, Aureta C. Keane

Library of Congress Cataloging-in-Publication Data

Keane, Nancy J.
 Middle school pathfinders : guiding student research / Nancy J. Keane.
   p. cm.
 Includes bibliographical references and index.
 ISBN 1-58683-200-X (pbk.)
 1. Library research--Handbooks, manuals, etc. 2. Internet
research--Handbooks, manuals, etc. 3. Library orientation for middle school
students--Handbooks, manuals, etc. 4. Bibliography--Methodology--Handbooks,
manuals, etc. 5. Web sites--Directories. I. Title.
Z710.K43 2005
025.5'24--dc22

                        2005013158

Author: **Nancy J. Keane**

Published by Linworth Publishing, Inc.
480 East Wilson Bridge Road, Suite L
Worthington, Ohio 43085

ISBN: 1-58683-200-X

5 4 3 2 1

Table of Contents

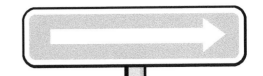

The Research Project 1

Social Studies 5
    Ancient Africa.. 7
    Ancient China 9
    Ancient Egypt 11
    Ancient Greece 13
    Ancient India... 15
    Ancient Rome 17
    Vikings 19
    Middle Ages 21
    Renaissance... 23
    Explorers 25
    Colonial America 27
    American Revolution 29
    U.S. Constitution.. 31
    Lewis and Clark 33
    Underground Railroad 35
    Civil War... 37
    Westward Expansion... 39
    Child Labor... 41
    Great Depression... 43
    World War I... 45
    World War II 47
    Civil Rights Movement... 49
    Martin Luther King, Jr. 51
    Countries/Travel 53
    Immigration... 55
    Native Americans History... 57
    Women's History 59
    African American History.. 61
    Hispanic American Culture.. 63
    U.S. Presidents 65
    World Religions 67

Science 69
    Physical Science
        Alternative Energy 71
        Chemical Elements 73
        Light and Optics 75
    Earth and Space Science
        Astronomy... 77
        Earthquakes 79
        El Niño 81
        Hurricanes 83
        Landforms 85
        Minerals... 87.
        Oceans 89
        Severe Weather 91

Table of Contents Continued

Tornadoes 93

Volcanoes..95

Life Science

Animals 97

Biomes..99

Endangered Species 101

Food Chain 103

Invasive Species 105

Nutrition 107

Rainforests 109

Science Fair Projects..111

Mathematics 113

Fractals 115

Mathematicians 117

Tessellations 119

Language 121

Folklore and Folktales 123

Mythology...125

Poetry 127

World Languages and Culture 129

Health 131

Drug Abuse 133

Genetic Diseases...135

Smoking and Tobacco...137

Music 139

Composers 141

Folk Music 143

Swing Era Music...145

Art..147

Artists 149

Technology Education 151

Bridges 153

Career Explorations 155

Consumer Education..157

Inventions and Inventors...159

Index 161

Acknowledgements

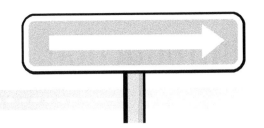

I wish to thank the people who have helped with this endeavor. My assistants, Sandy Soucy and Ruth Perencevich, have helped come up with topics and resources.

I would also like to thank the many librarians and teachers I have come in contact with. Their ideas and their willingness to share have helped a great deal. I am fortunate to work with a talented group of educators.

I would also like to thank my marvelous editor, Kathy Schrock. She has worked with me from the start of this manuscript offering advice and support. She is truly amazing!

Most importantly, I would like to thank my family—my children, Aureta and Alex, and my two fantastic grandsons who are a source of amazement and joy for me. Whenever I needed a break from writing, I simply spent time with the babies. They can always get me laughing!

About the Author

Nancy J. Keane is a school librarian in New Hampshire. She has been a lover a children's literature all her life, so working with books and children is a perfect match for her. In addition to her work in the school, Nancy also hosts a television show on local television. *Kids Book Beat*, is a monthly show that features children from the area booktalking their favorite books. The show also features local authors and storytellers. Nancy has also authored a children's fiction book and several books on using booktalks and literature across the curriculum. She writes a column about children's literature for her local newspaper.

Nancy is the author of an award winning Web site *Booktalks—Quick and Simple* (**http://www.nancykeane.com/booktalks**). The site logs about 30,000 hits a day and has proven to be indispensable to librarians and teachers. The database includes more than 3,000 ready-to-use booktalks and contributions are welcome from educators. Additionally, Nancy has a page of thematic booklists available on her page. *ATN Reading Lists* consists of about 1,900 thematic lists culled from suggestions from several professional e-mail discussion lists.

Nancy received a B.A. in child psychology from the University of Massachusetts, Amherst, an M.L.S. from University of Rhode Island, and an M.A. in Educational Technology from George Washington University. She is an adjunct faculty member at New Hampshire Technical College, Plymouth State University and teaches workshops for the University of New Hampshire. She also presents workshops at conferences.

Nancy has won numerous awards for her work. Awards include Winnebago Progressive Library Award, New Hampshire Educational Media Service Award, New Hampshire Excellence in Education Award, ALSC/Sagebrush Literature Programs for Children Award, and the Elizabeth Yates Literature Award.

Nancy lives in Concord, New Hampshire with her family. They share their home with an assortment of animals.

Introduction

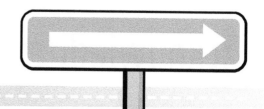

Library pathfinders have been around for quite a long time. Originally developed to help students create a path to their research by suggesting books to begin their investigation, they have now expanded to include Web sites as well. A pathfinder is not meant to be an exhaustive bibliographic guide to all that is available in the library. It is meant only as a guide to allow students to begin their research.

The pathfinders are useful in the middle school setting as many of the students need guidance to begin their research. There should be enough information to start the process but not so much that the student needs to do no research independently. Pathfinders allow a starting point and should suffice until more in-depth help is available from the teacher or the library media specialist.

In addition to listing print materials, the pathfinder helps the student with keywords, subject headings, Dewey numbers, and journal articles of interest. Web sites that contain good content information about the topic being studied are also included.

The creation of library pathfinders is rather labor-intensive. It takes hours of research to create each pathfinder. Ideally, library media specialists would create collection-specific pathfinders to aid their students in research. The reality of the situation is that many hard working library media specialists simply do not have the time to do this. So, they turn to commercially produced pathfinders and reproducible pathfinders such as this book. Since these pathfinders do not reflect the individual collection of each school library media center, the legitimate question is, do they have any value? I believe the answer is yes. Donna Miller, in her support of commercially produced pathfinders, states that "the user has at least a core group of materials with which to begin."[1] She goes on to estimate that it takes at least ten hours to create an in-house pathfinder.

The production of this book of pathfinders concentrates on topics normally taught at the middle school level. It is not meant to be a comprehensive list of pathfinders to cover every research topic in the middle school. As of March 2005, all books mentioned are in-print and all Web pages are correct and current. The Dewey numbers have been taken from *Dewey Decimal Classification Abridged*, edition 14, OCLC, 2004. Subject headings were taken from *Sears List of Subject Headings*, 16th edition, Wilson, 1997.

It is hoped that this work will allow middle school library media specialists to add another utensil to their cache of information literacy tools.

Nancy J. Keane

---

1 Miller, Donna. "Library Pathfinders." *Library Talk*. Mar/Apr 200, Vol. 13, Issue 2, p20

The Research Project

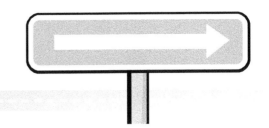

You've been assigned to do a research project. Now what? The first step is to stop and think about what you are going to do. Do not panic and try not to feel overwhelmed. If you give yourself enough time, the research project will be an interesting pursuit.

Finding a topic

The first thing you need to do is to find a topic. If your teacher has given you a list of topics to chose from, be sure to do a little thinking about them before you decide on your topic. Try to choose something that interests you. Think about the things you like to do and try to relate them to your topic. If you like to play computer games and have to do a research project on an ancient civilization, why not find out what types of games the children played? If you like sports, turn your American history project into a search for the types of sports that were played.

There are many places on the Internet that can help you chose your topic.

Hot Paper Topics
http://www.nwmissouri.edu/library/courses/english2/termindex.htm
This Web site is designed for students writing position or persuasive papers. It helps you break general topics into workable debate paper.

Idea Generator
http://www.lib.odu.edu/research/idea/ideagenerator.shtml
Browse through a variety of key words and phrases and then explore the ideas and devise a more specific topic.

Online Backgrounders from PBS
http://www.pbs.org/newshour/background.html
This Web site leads you to background reports from past programs. Some include segments of streaming video.

Developing a topic

Once you have chosen your project and your teacher has given you the go-ahead, it is time to start asking questions. Brainstorm some of the questions you have about your topic. If you don't have a lot of background knowledge about your topic, begin your research using the general encyclopedias. Look up your topic and start thinking about what more you would like to know about the topic. Also make note of specific keywords that can help you research further. Some Internet encyclopedias for you to use are:

Columbia Encyclopedia
http://www.bartleby.com/65/

Microsoft Encarta® Encyclopedia
http://www.encarta.com/

Encyclopedia.com
http://www.encyclopedia.com/

Find your sources

- After you have a good idea of what your topic is and what you need to know, you can then go further with your research. Begin by looking at the pathfinder available for your project. These are not exhaustive but offer starting locations for your research.

- Start your note-taking by getting down the hard facts. These include dates, statistics, scientific terms, formulas, etc. Reference books are the most likely place to find this type of information. You can also find information on the Internet if you look in the right place.

- Be sure to distinguish fact from opinion while researching. Opinion pieces are most likely to show up in periodical articles and on the Internet. These sources are ever-changing and may reflect temporary thinking.

- For doing research that involves in-depth information and a deeper understanding of the topic, books and scholarly journals are your best source of information. They are usually written by experts and will stand the test of time.

Evaluating Internet Resources

Not everything you find on the Internet is true or correct. The Internet is a wonderful source of information and very convenient as it can be accessed from home as well as school, but you need to be Internet savvy and not be taken in by bogus Web sites.

Points to consider when looking at a Web page:

Accuracy	• Does the information agree with what you already know? • Does the page contain blatant errors or typos? • How reliable and error-free is the information? • Is there evidence of bias? • Does the author have a specific agenda or point-of-view?
Authority	• Can you tell who is sponsoring the Web page? Is the sponsor legitimate? • Can you tell who wrote the page? • Are the qualifications of the author clearly stated? • Is the author affiliated with an institution or organization? • Is there contact information available for the author of the document?
Content	• Can you tell what the purpose of the web page is, i.e. to inform, convince, or sell? • Who is the intended audience? • What is the overall value of the content compared to the range of resources on the topic?
Currency	• Is the publication date clearly stated? • When was the page last revised? Is it maintained and updated regularly? • Are the links on the page up-to-date and useable?
Documentation	• Does the author explain where the information was obtained? • Does the Web page contain a bibliography or list of sources used? • Are there working links to the sources?

Citing Sources

When taking your notes, be extra careful to avoid plagiarism. You don't want to simply cut and paste from the Internet and then call the work your own. That is stealing. If caught, your teacher may give you a failing grade.

Since we all know a research paper relies on the work of others, it is important to cite your sources. This gives credit to those you have gathered your information from.

There are several standard methods used to cite sources and your teacher or librarian will help you find what is acceptable in your school. There are several web pages available to help you as well.

Your best source of all for any research is your library media specialist. Library media specialists are trained to help with research and have lots of experience.

Using MLA Style to Cite and Document Sources
http://www.bedfordstmartins.com/online/cite5.html

OWL Online Writing Lab
http://owl.english.purdue.edu/handouts/research/r_mla.html#Works-Cited

EasyBib
http://www.easybib.com/

Citation Machine—The Landmark Project
http://www.landmark-project.com/citation_machine/index.php
The principal goal of this tool is to make the proper crediting of information property so easy that it becomes a habit, not a laborious task that we stop doing outside of school.

NoodleBib Starter (Free Version)
http://www.noodletools.com/noodlebib/index.php
MLA Starter gives the student clear, color-coded examples of how to cite the sources they are most likely to encounter (printed and online books, reference sources, magazines, newspapers, etc.).

Topic: Ancient Africa

Pathfinders are guides which are intended to help you get started doing research on a particular topic, both online and at your library. Although these resources are useful as a starting point for your research, they are not the only resources that are available to you.

Definition/Introduction

- ### *What is the topic? What does it cover?*

    Once called "the Dark Continent,", Africa has seen its share of civilizations come and go. In this unit, the student will learn about the people who have called Africa home.

- ### *Catalog Subject Headings or Keywords*

    Africa
    Ancient civilization
    Ancient history
    > *See also names of ancient peoples residing in Africa.*

- ### *Dewey Numbers*

    930 Ancient history
    939 Ancient Africa
    960 Africa

Print Resources

- ### *Reference titles [dictionaries, encyclopedias, atlases, specific subject references]*

    Africa: An Encyclopedia for Students. Charles Scribner's Sons , Gale Group/Thomson Learning, c2002.

    African History on File. Facts On File, c2003.

    Bianchi, Robert Steven. *Daily Life of the Nubians.* Greenwood Press, c2004.

    Encyclopedia of African Peoples. Facts On File, c2000.

    Farrington, Karen. *Historical Atlas of Expeditions.* Checkmark Books, c2000.

- ### *General titles [nonfiction, any suitable fiction]*

    Be sure to check the library online catalog to find additional suitable materials.

    Service, Pamela F. *300 B.C.* Benchmark Books/Marshall Cavendish, c2003.

    Service, Pamela F. *The Ancient African Kingdom of the Kush.* Benchmark Books, 1998.

    Somervill, Barbara A. *Empires of Ancient West Africa (Great Empires of the Past).* Facts On File, c2004.

■ *Journals*

Be sure to check any online periodical database at your school library for more.

Hanson-Harding, Alexandra. "African Kingdoms". *Junior Scholastic*, 02/07/2000, Vol. 102 Issue 12, p10, 4p, 5c

McCollum, Sean. "African Queens". *Junior Scholastic*, 3/8/2004, Vol. 106 Issue 14, p15, 3p, 1 map, 2c

Web Resources

Ancient Africa
http://www.mrdowling.com/609ancafr.html
Special sections in this site include: The Nok, The Phoenicians, Carthage, Ghana, Sudiata, Mansa, Musa, Timbuktu, Zimbabwe, and Trade in Ancient Africa.

African Civilizations in the Classical Era (Axial age) in 1000-600 A.D.
http://www.stockton.edu/~gilmorew/consorti/1cafric.htm
This time period marked a very dynamic and turbulent era in Africa's history.

African Voices
http://www.mnh.si.edu/africanvoices/
The Smithsonian Natural History Web has a timeline of events from Prehistory to today related to Africa.

Mystery of the Great Zimbabwe
http://www.pbs.org/wgbh/nova/israel/zimbabwe.html
Nova Online is responsible for this site that explains and explores the ruins of Zimbabwe.

Wonders of the African World
http://www.pbs.org/wonders/
This site provides information on Nubia, Swahili, Slave Kingdoms, The Holy Land, and the Road to Timbuktu.

Topic: Ancient China

Middle School Library Pathfinder

Pathfinders are guides which are intended to help you get started doing research on a particular topic, both online and at your library. Although these resources are useful as a starting point for your research, they are not the only resources that are available to you.

Definition/Introduction

- ### *What is the topic? What does it cover?*

  The country of China has a long and distinguished history. The study of Ancient China covers the history through the year 420.

- ### *Catalog Subject Headings or Keywords*

  China
  Ancient civilizations
  Ancient history

- ### *Dewey Numbers*

  930 Ancient history
  931 Ancient China
  951 China

Print Resources

- ### *Reference titles [dictionaries, encyclopedias, atlases, specific subject references]*

  Higham, Charles. *Encyclopedia of Ancient Asian Civilizations*. Facts On File, c2004.

  Knight, Judson. *Ancient Civilizations*. UXL, c2000.

- ### *General titles [nonfiction, any suitable fiction]*

  Be sure to check the library online catalog to find additional suitable materials.

  Allison, Amy. *Life In Ancient China*. Lucent Books, c2001.

  Anderson, Dale. *Ancient China*. Raintree, c2005.

  Baldwin, Robert F. *Daily Life In Ancient and Modern Beijing*. Runestone Press, c1999.

  Cotterell, Arthur. *Ancient China*. DK Publishing, c2000.

  Hammond, Paula. *China and Japan*. Mason Crest Publishers, c2003.

  Leon, Vicki. *Outrageous Women of Ancient Times*. John Wiley, c1998.

  O'Connor, Jane. *The Emperor's Silent Army: Terracotta Warriors of Ancient China*. Viking, c2002.

  Rees, Rosemary. *The Ancient Chinese*. Heinemann Library, c2002.

  Tracy, Kathleen. *The Life and Times of Confucius*. Mitchell Lane Publishers, c2005.

  Wells, Donald. *The Silk Road*. Weigl Publishers, c2005.

■ *Journals*

Be sure to check any online periodical database at your school library for more.

"Ancient China Timeline". *Events of Ancient Civilization*, 2002, p51, 4p

Bossler, Beverly. "Women's Lives in the Song Dynasty". Calliope, Dec2002, Vol. 13 Issue 4, p26, 3p, 2c, 3bw

"Finding the Past in the Present". *Kids Discover*, Apr97, Vol. 7 Issue 4, p16, 2p, 10c

"How the Rich Lived". *Kids Discover*, Apr97, Vol. 7 Issue 4, p6, 1p, 6c

"The Peasant Poor". *Kids Discover*, Apr97, Vol. 7 Issue 4, p7, 1p, 7c

Steinhardt, Nancy S... "How a Song Builder Knew What To Build". *Calliope*, Dec2002, Vol. 13 Issue 4, p18, 2p, 3 diagrams

Web Resources

China: 5,000 Years
http://www.guggenheim.org/exhibitions/past_exhibitions/china/rotunda.html
China: 5,000 Years is the result of collaboration between the Guggenheim Museum and the Ministry of Culture and the National Administration for Cultural Heritage of the People's Republic of China.

China Daily Life
http://www.historylink101.com/china/china_daily_life.htm
Links to many pages about China and its history.

Chinese Inventions and Remedies
http://www.crystalinks.com/chinainventions.html
Some of the greatest inventions in the world were made by the Chinese. Learn about some of them here.

History Timeline
http://www-chaos.umd.edu/history/time_line.html
Clicking on the Chinese characters for each of the dynasties will bring up a list of the emperors (in Chinese) for each of the respective dynasties.

Portraits of Chinese Emperors
http://www.chinapage.com/emperor.html
Listed in chronological order.

Topic: Ancient Eygpt

Pathfinders are guides which are intended to help you get started doing research on a particular topic, both online and at your library. Although these resources are useful as a starting point for your research, they are not the only resources that are available to you.

Definition/Introduction

■ *What is the topic? What does it cover?*

The history of Egypt is fascinating to study. With the pyramids, the mummies and all the mysteries that go with them, it is exciting to learn about. The study of Ancient Egypt covers the time period to approximately 640 A.D.

■ *Catalog Subject Headings or Keywords*

Egypt
Ancient civilization
Ancient history

■ *Dewey Numbers*

930 Ancient history
932 Ancient Eygpt
962 Egypt

Print Resources

■ *Reference titles [dictionaries, encyclopedias, atlases, specific subject references]*

Arts & Humanities Through the Eras. Ancient Egypt, 2675-332 B.C.E. Thomson/Gale, c2005.

Baines, John. *Cultural Atlas of Ancient Egypt.* Facts On File, c2000.

Bunson, Margaret. *Encyclopedia of Ancient Egypt.* Facts On File, c2002.

Knight, Judson. *Ancient Civilizations.* UXL, c2000.

Netzley, Patricia D. *The Greenhaven Encyclopedia of Ancient Egypt.* Greenhaven Press , Thomson/Gale, c2003.

■ *General titles [nonfiction, any suitable fiction]*

Be sure to check the library online catalog to find additional suitable materials.

Chrisp, Peter. *Ancient Egypt Revealed.* DK Publishing, c2002.

Day, Nancy. *Your Travel Guide to Ancient Egypt.* Runestone, c2001.

Defrates, Joanna. *What Do We Know About the Egyptians?* P. Bedrick Books, c1992.

Harris, Geraldine. *Ancient Egypt.* Facts On File, c2003.

Jovinelly, Joann. *The Crafts and Culture of the Ancient Egyptians.* Rosen Central, 2002.

Morley, Jacqueline. *How Would You Survive as an Ancient Egyptian?* Franklin Watts, 1995, 1993.

Nardo, Don. *Ancient Egypt*. Lucent Books, Thomson/Gale, c2003.

Perl, Lila. *Mummies, Tombs, and Treasure: Secrets of Ancient Egypt*. Clarion Books, c1987.

Rees, Rosemary. *The Ancient Egyptians*. Heinemann Library, c1997.

■ *Journals*

Be sure to check any online periodical database at your school library for more.

Brovarski, Edward. "The Egyptians at Play". *Calliope*, Sep2001, Vol. 12 Issue 1, p24, 2p, 1c

Brown, Bryan. "New Discoveries in Ancient Egypt". *Junior Scholastic*, 9/6/2004, Vol. 107 Issue 1, p18, 2p, 1 map, 2c

"Daily Life". *Kids Discover*, Sep2001, Vol. 11 Issue 9, p6, 2p, 7c

Landauro, Victor. "Life in Ancient Egypt". (cover story) *Junior Scholastic*, 9/6/2002, Vol. 105 Issue 1, p9, 3p, 4c

"More on Ancient Egypt". *Kids Discover*, Sep2001, Vol. 11 Issue 9, p18, 1/5p

Smith, Steph. "A Peek Inside a Mummy". *Scholastic News—Senior Edition*, 10/25/2002, Vol. 71 Issue 7, p6, 1p, 2c

"Treasures From Egypt"s Past". *National Geographic*, Jun2004, Vol. 205 Issue 6, Preceding p1, 1/4p, 1c

Web Resources

Ancient Egypt History
http://touregypt.net/egyptantiquities/
Information about the history of Egypt. Ancient Egypt was a land of firsts and this site discusses many of the firsts.

The British Museum Ancient Egypt site
http://www.ancientegypt.co.uk/menu.html
Information about Egyptian life, geography, gods and goddesses, mummification, pharaohs, pyramids, and much more.

Cyber Mummy
http://archive.ncsa.uiuc.edu/Cyberia/VideoTestbed/Projects/Mummy/mummyhome.html
Unlock its secrets with the help of modern medical imagery, a supercomputer, and an archeologist.

Egypt – Gift of the Nile
http://www.seattleartmuseum.org/Exhibit/Archive/egypt/default.htm
From an exhibit at the Seattle Art Museum, October 15, 1998-January 10, 1999.

Life in Ancient Egypt
http://www.carnegiemuseums.org/cmnh/exhibits/egypt/
"In the hall the artifacts are displayed in relation to the daily life and traditions of the people who made them, so that the objects are seen in the context of the culture."

Topic: Ancient Greece

Middle School Library Pathfinder

Pathfinders are guides which are intended to help you get started doing research on a particular topic, both online and at your library. Although these resources are useful as a starting point for your research, they are not the only resources that are available to you.

Definition/Introduction

- ### What is the topic? What does it cover?

  The country of Greece is the home to the original Olympics, the Parthenon, and the birthplace of many important scientists, mathematicians and writers. The study of Ancient Greece generally looks at the country to approximately 323 A.D.

- ### Catalog Subject Headings or Keywords

  Greece
  Ancient history
  Ancient civilization

- ### Dewey Numbers

  930 Ancient history
  938 Ancient Greece
  949.5 Greece

Print Resources

- ### Reference titles [dictionaries, encyclopedias, atlases, specific subject references]

  Adkins, Lesley. *Handbook to Life in Ancient Greece.* Oxford University Press, c1998.

  Ancient Greece and Rome: An Encyclopedia For Students. Charles Scribner's Sons, c1998.

  The Encyclopedia of Ancient Civilizations of the Near East and Mediterranean. Sharpe Reference, c1997.

  Sacks, David. *Encyclopedia of the Ancient Greek World.* Facts On File, c1995.

  Sheehan, Sean., *Illustrated Encyclopedia of Ancient Greece.* J. Paul Getty Museum, c2002.

- ### General titles [nonfiction, any suitable fiction]

  Be sure to check the library online catalog to find additional suitable materials.

  Day, Nancy. *Your Travel Guide to Ancient Greece.* Runestone, c2001.

  Jovinelly, Joann. *The Crafts and Culture of the Ancient Greeks.* Rosen Central, c2002.

  Nardo, Don. *Ancient Athens.* Lucent Books , Thomson/Gale, c2003.

  Nardo, Don. *Ancient Greece.* Lucent Books , Thomson/Gale, c2003.

  Pearson, Anne. *What Do We Know About the Greeks?* P. Bedrick Books, c1992.

  Powell, Anton. *Ancient Greece.* Facts On File, c2003.

Rees, Rosemary. *The Ancient Greeks.* Heinemann Library, c1997.

Woff, Richard. *Bright-Eyed Athena: Stories From Ancient Greece.* J. Paul Getty Museum, c1999.

■ Journals

Be sure to check any online periodical database at your school library for more.

Brown, Bryan. "Ancient Greece". *Junior Scholastic,* 10/18/2004, Vol. 107 Issue 4, P18, 4p, 1 map, 4c, 1bw

"Digging Up the Past". *Kids Discover,* Aug/Sep94, Vol. 4 Issue 7, P16, 2p, 8c, 1bw

Digiorgio, Michael. "The World of Ancient Greece". *Calliope,* Nov97, Vol. 8 Issue 3, P4, 2p

Dixon, Pam. "The Beginning of Democracy". *Calliope,* Nov/Dec94, Vol. 5 Issue 2, P5, 6p, 20bw

"Great Greece!" *Kids Discover,* Aug/Sep94, Vol. 4 Issue 7, P2, 2p, 16c, 1bw

Web Resources

The Ancient Greek World
http://www.museum.upenn.edu/Greek_World/index2.html
Ancient Greek World virtual gallery at the University of Pennsylvania Museum of Archaeology and Anthropology.

Ancient Greeks
http://www.arwhead.com/Greeks/
Short, illustrated examples of Ancient Greek life and culture.

Encyclopedia of Greek Mythology
http://www.mythweb.com/encyc/
Lots of information about Greek mythology.

The Greeks
http://www.pbs.org/empires/thegreeks/
Part of the PBS Empires series. EMPIRES® is a ground breaking series of epic historical films, which present the people and passions that have changed the world.

Odyssey Online – Greece
http://www.carlos.emory.edu/ODYSSEY/GREECE/homepg.html
"In this section of Odyssey Online, we"ll look at ancient Greek objects to learn more about the people who made and used them, the rich culture of these people, and their legacy in our lives today."

Topic: Ancient India

Middle School Library Pathfinder

Pathfinders are guides which are intended to help you get started doing research on a particular topic, both online and at your library. Although these resources are useful as a starting point for your research, they are not the only resources that are available to you.

Definition/Introduction

■ *What is the topic? What does it cover?*

The study of ancient India is mainly the study of a mystery. Little is known about the civilizations that inhabited the area now known as India. The excavation of the city of Harappa revealed a highly evolved civilization that vanished about 1500 B.C. What is known about ancient India is fascinating to study.

■ *Catalog Subject Headings or Keywords*

India
Indus River
South Asia
Ganges River
Ancient civilization
Ancient history

■ *Dewey Numbers*

930 General Ancient history
934 Ancient India
954 India

Print Resources

■ *Reference titles [dictionaries, encyclopedias, atlases, specific subject references]*

Great civilizations of the East: Discover the Rremarkable History of Asia and the Far East: Mesopotamia, Ancient India, the Chinese Empire, Ancient Japan. London: Southwater Press; c2001.

■ *General titles [nonfiction, any suitable fiction]*

Be sure to check the library online catalog to find additional suitable materials.

Ali, Daud. *Ancient India: What Life Was Like For the Ancient Indians.* Southwater, Distributed by National Book Network, c2003.

Schomp, Virginia. *Ancient India (People of the Ancient World).* Franklin Watts, c2005.

Woods, Michael. *Ancient Warfare: From Clubs to Catapults.* Runestone, c2000.

■ *Journals*

Be sure to check any online periodical database at your school library for more.

Browne, Eric [et al.] "India". *Monkeyshines on Ancient Cultures*, 2001, p83, 7p

"Mysterious Ancient India". *Kids Discover*, May2003, Vol. 13 Issue 5, p2, 2p, 1 map, 5c

Souci, Robert D. San. "The Hunas in India". *Calliope*, Sep/Oct91, Vol. 2 Issue 1, p20, 4p, 3bw

Web Resources

Ancient India
http://www.mnsu.edu/emuseum/prehistory/india/index.shtml
Geography and Origins of Ancient Indus Civilization; Cultural Elements and Timeline of the Harappan; Arts Technology and Trade of the Classical Harappan.

The Ancient Indus Valley
http://www.harappa.com/har/har0.html
1,001 illustrated pages by the world's leading scholars.

The British Museum
http://www.ancientindia.co.uk/index.html
This site addresses themes or topics relevant to ancient India.

A Country Study: India
http://lcweb2.loc.gov/frd/cs/intoc.html
Prepared by the Federal Research Division of the Library of Congress under the Country Studies/Area Handbook Program sponsored by the Department of the Army.

Daily Life in Ancient India
http://members.aol.com/Donnclass/Indialife.html
"This site shares daily life in three major time periods of ancient India history; the mysterious and so cool Indus Valley Civilization, the Vedic & Epics Periods, and the Age of Empires."

Harappan Civilization ca. 3000-1500 B.C.
http://campus.northpark.edu/history//WebChron/India/Harappa.html
One of the most fascinating yet mysterious cultures of the ancient world is the Harappan civilization. This culture existed along the Indus River.

Timeline of Indian Art
http://www.kamat.com/kalranga/art/timeline.htm
Paintings, Architecture, and Fine Art in India Through the Centuries.

Topic: Ancient Rome

Middle School Library Pathfinder

Pathfinders are guides which are intended to help you get started doing research on a particular topic, both online and at your library. Although these resources are useful as a starting point for your research, they are not the only resources that are available to you.

Definition/Introduction

- *What is the topic? What does it cover?*

   The story of ancient Rome is the story of how a small community became one of the world's greatest empires. Ancient Rome had an enormous influence on the development of Western civilization.

- *Catalog Subject Headings or Keywords*

   Rome
   Italy
   Ancient civilization
   Ancient history

- *Dewey Numbers*

   930 Ancient history
   937 Ancient Rome
   945 Italy

Print Resources

- *Reference titles [dictionaries, encyclopedias, atlases, specific subject references]*

   Adkins, Lesley. *Handbook to Life in Ancient Rome.* Facts On File, c2004.

   Ancient Greece and Rome: An Encyclopedia for Students. Charles Scribner's Sons, c1998.

   Arts & Humanities Through the Eras. Ancient Greece and Rome, 1200 B.C.E.-476 C.E. Thomson/Gale, c2005.

   Corbishley, Mike. *Illustrated Encyclopedia of Ancient Rome.* J. Paul Getty Museum, c2004, c2003.

   Knight, Judson. *Ancient Civilizations.* UXL, c2000.

   Nardo, Don. *The Greenhaven Encyclopedia of Ancient Rome.* Greenhaven Press, c2002.

- *General titles [nonfiction, any suitable fiction]*

   Be sure to check the library online catalog to find additional suitable materials.

   Corbishley, Mike. *Ancient Rome.* Facts On File, c2003.

   Ganeri, Anita. *How Would You Survive as an Ancient Roman?* Franklin Watts, c1995, c1993.

   Grant, Neil. *Every Day Life in Ancient Rome.* Smart Apple Media, c2004.

   Jovinelly, Joann. *The Crafts and Culture of the Romans.* Rosen Central, c2002.

   Lassieur, Allison. *The Ancient Romans.* Franklin Watts, c2004.

Markel, Rita J. *Your Travel Guide To Ancient Rome.* Lerner Publications Co., c2004.

Mellor, Ronalld. *The Ancient Roman World.* Oxford University Press, c2004.

Nardo, Don. *The Ancient Romans.* Lucent Books, c2001.

Nardo, Don. *Women of Ancient Rome.* Lucent Books , Thomson/Gale, c2003.

Woods, Michael. *Ancient Warfare: From Clubs to Catapults.* Runestone, c2000.

■ *Journals*

Be sure to check any online periodical database at your school library for more.

Bianchi, Robert Steven. "The Ancient Mediterranean". *Faces*, Oct95, Vol. 12 Issue 2, p6, 4p, 4bw

Hambleton, Vicki. "The Wonders of Ancient Rome". *Calliope*, Jan2001, Vol. 11 Issue 5, p44, 4p, 1c

Hanson-Harding, Alexandra. "If You Lived in Ancient Rome". *Junior Scholastic,* 12/10/2001, Vol. 104 Issue 9, p14, 4p, 1 map, 5c

"Poor Life". *Kids Discover*, Aug/Sep93, Vol. 3 Issue 7, p8, 2p, 3c

"Rich Life". *Kids Discover*, Aug/Sep93, Vol. 3 Issue 7, p12, 2p, 8c

Web Resources

Daily Life in Rome
http://www.uvm.edu/~classics/webresources/life/hist.html
Information about Roman history including timeline.

De Imperatoribus Romanis: An Online Encyclopedia of Roman Emperors
http://www.roman-emperors.org/
Online encyclopedia on the rulers of the Roman empire from Augustus to Constantine XI Palaeologus.

Dead Romans
http://www.deadromans.com/
"Salve amice! Welcome to Dead Romans, a work-in-progress that features information about Roman coins, architecture, and artwork from the Early Roman Empire."

History for Kids
http://www.historyforkids.org/learn/romans/index.htm
Information about Ancient Rome including a time line, the environment, religion, clothing, language, food, science, people, and more.

Maps of the Roman Empire
http://intranet.dalton.org/groups/rome/RMAPS.html
Many maps including trade routes.

Topic: Ancient Vikings

Middle School Library Pathfinder

Pathfinders are guides which are intended to help you get started doing research on a particular topic, both online and at your library. Although these resources are useful as a starting point for your research, they are not the only resources that are available to you.

Definition/Introduction

■ *What is the topic? What does it cover?*

Vikings were medieval Scandinavian sea warriors who traded with and raided Europe from the 8th through the 11th centuries. They often settled in the countries they invaded and therefore their influence is felt throughout Europe.

■ *Catalog Subject Headings or Keywords*

Vikings
Norsemen
Scandinavians
Normans

■ *Dewey Numbers*

948   Vikings
936.3   Ancient history

Print Resources

■ *Reference titles [dictionaries, encyclopedias, atlases, specific subject references]*

Konstam, Angus. *Historical Atlas of the Viking World.* Checkmark Books, c2002.

Morley, Jacqueline. *First Facts About the Vikings.* P. Bedrick Books, c1996.

■ *General titles [nonfiction, any suitable fiction]*

Be sure to check the library online catalog to find additional suitable materials.

Berger, Melvin. *The Real Vikings: Craftsmen, Traders, and Fearsome Raiders.* National Geographic Society, c2003.

James, John. *How We Know About the Vikings.* P. Bedrick Books, c1997.

Kimmel, Elizabeth Cody. *Before Columbus: The Leif Eriksson Expedition.* Random House, c2003.

Philip, Neil. *Odin's Family: Myths of the Vikings.* Orchard Books, c1996.

■ *Journals*

Be sure to check any online periodical database at your school library for more.

Childress, Diana. "An English Victory at the Bridge". *Calliope,* Feb2001, Vol. 11 Issue 6, p15, 1p, 1c

"Explorers and Traders". *Kids Discover,* Nov95, Vol. 5 Issue 9, p4, 2p, 6c, 2bw

"How Vikings Lived". *Time for Kids*, 02/28/97, Vol. 2 Issue 19, p6, 1p, 2c

"In Days of Old". *Kids Discover*, Dec2003, Vol. 13 Issue 12, p2, 2p, 5c, 1bw

Kowalski, Kathiann M. "Anglo-Saxons Unite Against The Viking Threat". *Calliope*, Feb2001, Vol. 11 Issue 6, p7, 3p, 2c

Linden, Eugene. "The Vikings: A Memorable Visit To America". *Smithsonian*, Dec2004, Vol. 35 Issue 9, p92, 7p, 1 map, 7c

"Meet the Vikings". *Calliope*, Nov/Dec92, Vol. 3 Issue 2, p44, 2p, 1 chart, 2bw

Ryan, James. "Leif Ericson". *People of the Middle Ages*, 2002, p7, 2p

Web Resources

Nova – The Vikings
http://www.pbs.org/wgbh/nova/vikings/
Companion Web site to "The Vikings," a two-hour NOVA program originally broadcast on May 9, 2000. The program examines a new, less barbarian image of the Norsemen based on recent archeological investigations.

Vikings – The North Atlantic Saga
http://www.mnh.si.edu/vikings/start.html
From the rise of the Scandinavian kingdoms during the Viking Age (A.D. 750 to 1050) to the demise of the Greenland colonies around A.D. 1500, *Vikings: The North Atlantic Saga* examines the history of the western expansion of the Vikings and sheds new light on a well-known culture.

The Vikings
http://www.cdli.ca/CITE/vikings.htm
Lots of information about the Vikings from the Gander Academy in Gander, Newfoundland.

The Vikings
http://www.cdli.ca/CITE/vikings.htm
Article by Arne Emil Christensen about the history of the Vikings.

The Vikings
http://www.midcoast.com.au/~ttc/viking.html
Learn about ancient Viking culture, including religion, food, music, clothes, housing, law, money, everyday life, and more.

Topic: Middle Ages

Pathfinders are guides which are intended to help you get started doing research on a particular topic, both online and at your library. Although these resources are useful as a starting point for your research, they are not the only resources that are available to you.

Definition/Introduction

- ### *What is the topic? What does it cover?*

    The Middle Ages stretched from the 5th century to the 15th century. It began with the end of the Roman Empire and lasted until the age of the Renaissance.

- ### *Catalog Subject Headings or Keywords*

    Middle ages
    Castles
    Knights and knighthood
    Medieval

- ### *Dewey Numbers*

    909.07 World history from ca. 500 to 1500
    940.1   History of Europe from earliest history to 1453

Print Resources

- ## *Reference titles [dictionaries, encyclopedias, atlases, specific subject references]*

    The Expanding World. Facts On File, c1999.

    Lawler, Jennifer. *Encyclopedia of Women In The Middle Ages.* McFarland, c2001.

    The Middle Ages: An Encyclopedia for Students. Charles Scribner's Sons, Simon & Schuster and Prentice Hall International, c1996.

    Streissguth, Thomas. *The Greenhaven Encyclopedia of The Middle Ages.* Greenhaven Press, Thomson/Gale, c2003.

    Timelines On File. The Ancient and Medieval World, (Prehistory-1500 CE). Facts On File, c2000.

- ## *General titles [nonfiction, any suitable fiction]*

    Be sure to check the library online catalog to find additional suitable materials.

    Corbishley, Mike. *The Middle Ages.* Facts On File, c2003.

    Hinds, Kathryn. *Life in the Middle Ages. The Castle.* Benchmark Books, c2001.

    Hinds, Kathryn. *Life in the Middle Ages. The Church.* Benchmark Books, c2001.

    Hinds, Kathryn. *Life in the Middle Ages. The City.* Benchmark Books, c2001.

    Hinds, Kathryn. *Life in the Middle Ages. The Countryside.* Benchmark Books, c2001.

    Macdonald, Fiona. *Warfare in the Middle Ages.* P. Bedrick Books, c2004, c2003.

■ *Journals*

Be sure to check the online periodical database at your school library for more.

Grasset, Constance Dedie. "The Middle Ages". *Faces*, May93, Vol. 9 Issue 9, p14, 3p, 2bw

Orme, Nicholas. "Child's Play in Medieval England". *History Today*, Oct2001, Vol. 51 Issue 10, p49, 7p, 15c

Price, Sean. "If You Live in Medieval Times". *Junior Scholastic*, 12/01/97, Vol. 100 Issue 8, p14, 4p, 4c

Web Resources

The Camelot International Village
http://www.camelotintl.com/
Click on the different people in the street to learn more about their craft or trade and how they lived in the Middle Ages.

Internet Medieval Sourcebook
http://www.fordham.edu/halsall/sbook.html
Comprehensive collection of online texts from the entire medieval era, organized by topic and chronologically.

Medieval English Towns
http://www.trytel.com/%7Etristan/towns/towns.html
This in-depth site focuses on "medieval boroughs of East Anglia and social, political and constitutional history."

Medieval Technology Pages
http://scholar.chem.nyu.edu/tekpages/Technology.html
This site provides information on technological innovations and related subjects in western Europe during the Middle Ages, by subject or by timeline.

Medieval Timeline Reference
http://www.timeref.com
"A database of medieval events, people and places." Includes a timeline, people, places, maps, family trees, and more.

Middle Ages
http://www.learner.org/exhibits/middleages/
Everyday life in medieval times including feudal life, religion, clothes, the arts, and more.

The Middle Ages
http://www.scotttrees.com/middleages/
Discover feudalism and what life was like for peasants, soldiers, barons, and the royal court.

Topic: Renaissance

Definition/Introduction

■ *What is the topic? What does it cover?*

The term Renaissance, describing the period of European history from the early 14th to the late 16th century, is derived from the French word for rebirth. It originally referred to the revival of the values and artistic styles of classical antiquity during that period, especially in Italy.

■ *Catalog Subject Headings or Keywords*

Middle Ages history
> *See also the names of individuals associated with the Renaissance and names of individual countries.*

■ *Dewey Numbers*

909 World history
912 Maps
940.2 History of Europe, 1453-
940-949 History of Europe
950-959 History of Asia
960-969 History of Africa

Print Resources

■ *Reference titles [dictionaries, encyclopedias, atlases, specific subject references]*

Arts & Humanities Through the Eras. Renaissance Europe, 1300-1600. Thomson/Gale, c2005.

Encyclopedia of the Renaissance and the Reformation. Facts On File, c2004.

Extraordinary Women of the Medieval and Renaissance World: A Biographical Dictionary. Greenwood Press, c2000.

The Renaissance: An Encyclopedia for Students. Charles Scribner's Sons, Thomson/Gale, c2004.

Renaissance & Reformation. UXL, Thomson/Gale, c2002.

■ *General titles [nonfiction, any suitable fiction]*

Be sure to check the library online catalog to find additional suitable materials.

Barter, James. *Artists of the Renaissance.* Lucent Books, c1999.

Cole, Alison. *Renaissance.* DK Publishing, c2000.

Day, Nancy. *Your Travel Guide to Renaissance Europe.* Runestone, c2001.

Netzley, Patricia D. *Life During the Renaissance.* Lucent Books, c1998.

■ *Journals*

Be sure to check the online periodical database in your school library for more.

Conover, Kirsten. "Step into the 16th century". *Christian Science Monitor*, 11/14/2000, Vol. 92 Issue 248, p18, 0p, 2c

Day, Nancy. "A Time Of Discovery And Rediscovery". *Calliope*, May/Jun94, Vol. 4 Issue 5, p4, 6p, 4bw

Foote, Timothy. "Where Columbus Was Coming From". *Smithsonian,* Dec91, Vol. 22 Issue 9, p28, 13p, 13c, 1bw

Hong, Karen E. "The Legacy of the Medici". *Calliope*, Apr2001, Vol. 11 Issue 8, p44, 2p, 2c

Hughes, Robert. "Mighty Medici". *Time*, 12/9/2002, Vol. 160 Issue 24, p92, 2p, 5c

Skomal, Susan. "Arts and Statecraft Thrive in Europe: 1350-1600". *World Almanac & Book of Facts*, 2004, p465, 2p, 2bw

Web Resources

Artists by Movement: The Early Renaissance
http://www.artcyclopedia.com/history/early-renaissance.html
Chronological listing of early Renaissance artists.

Renaissance
http://www.learner.org/exhibits/renaissance/
"Explore the Renaissance and discover the forces that drove this rebirth in Europe, and in Italy in particular."

Renaissance Sites
http://renaissance.dm.net/sites.html
Links to information about the people, literature, food, games, guilds, and more.

Renaissance: The Elizabethan World
http://renaissance.dm.net/
Links to information about life during the Elizabethan period.

Welcome to the Renaissance Faire
http://www.renfaire.com/index.html
"Step back 400 years to a time of Romance. Shakespeare is in the prime of his career. Sir Francis Drake has circumnavigated the Globe. The New World exists as a boundless frontier. The Dark Ages are done. Fiat Lux."

Topic: Explorers

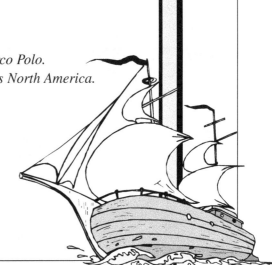

Definition/Introduction

■ *What is the topic? What does it cover?*

Once of the most common activities for humans is to explore. We are constantly exploring our surroundings. When we think of explorers and exploration, we usually think about people who go into uncharted places to find out what is there. In this unit, we will study the people who set off to explore new lands on our own planet.

■ *Catalog Subject Headings or Keywords*

Discoveries
Explorers
Exploration
Expedition
   See also names of individual explorers, such as Marco Polo.
   See also names of specific geographic areas, such as North America.

■ *Dewey Numbers*

910 Geography and travel
910.9 Explorers and discoveries
917.04 Geography and travel in North America
919.8 Geography and travel—other areas
920 Collective biography
970.01 General History—North America

Print Resources

■ *Reference titles [dictionaries, encyclopedias, atlases, specific subject references]*

Farrington, Karen. *Historical Atlas of Expeditions.* Checkmark Books, c2000.

Netzley, Patricia D. *Encyclopedia of Women's Travel and Exploration.* Oryx Press, c2001.

Waldman, Carl. *Encyclopedia of Exploration.* Facts On File, c2004.

Explorers: From Ancient Times to the Space Age. Macmillan Reference USA, Simon & Schuster and Prentice Hall International, c1999.

Geography And Exploration: Biographical Portraits. Charles Scribner's Sons, c2002.

Social Studies

■ *General titles [nonfiction, any suitable fiction]*

Be sure to check the library online catalog to find additional suitable materials.

Bernhard, Brendan. *Pizarro, Orellana, and the Exploration of the Amazon.* Chelsea House, c1991.

Brennan, Kristine. *Sir Edmund Hillary, Modern-Day Explorer.* Chelsea House, c2001.

Kimmel, Elizabeth Cody. *Before Columbus: The Leif Eriksson Expedition.* Random House, c2003.

Levinson, Nancy Smiler. *Magellan and the First Voyage Around the World.* Clarion Books, c2001.

Pella, Kathy. *Discovering Christopher Columbus: How History is Invented.* Lerner Publications, c1991.

Schraff, Anne E. *American Heroes of Exploration and Flight.* Enslow Publishers, c1996..

■ *Journals*

Be sure to check any online periodical database at your school library for more.

"Discovering America". *American History & Politics, 1607-1849*, 2002, p13, 2p

Hsu, Caroline. "The Chinese Columbus?" *U.S. News & World Report*, 2/23/2004, Vol. 136 Issue 7, p56, 4p, 4c

McClure, Larry. "Explorers & Pioneers". *Cobblestone*, Apr2004, Vol. 25 Issue 4, p2, 3p, 3c

Millman, Lawrence. "Looking for Henry Hudson". *Smithsonian*, Oct99, Vol. 30 Issue 7, p100, 10p, 5c

Web Resources

Explorers—A to Z
http://www.42explore2.com/explorers2.htm
Listing of biography sites for explorers.

Explorers from the 1600s to the Seventeenth Century
http://www.enchantedlearning.com/explorers/1600.shtml
Indexed alphabetically, by time period and by location.

Kid Info
http://www.kidinfo.com/American_History/Explorers.html
Links to pages about famous explorers.

The Mariners' Museum – Age of Exploration
http://www.mariner.org//educationalad/ageofex/
Includes information about maritime discovery from ancient times to Captain Cook's 1768 voyage to the South Pacific.

Multnomah County Library Homework Center
http://www.multcolib.org/homework/alphaexp.html
Alphabetical list of explorers.

Primary Sources
http://www.win.tue.nl/~engels/discovery/primary.html
Primary sources on voyages of discovery that can be found on the Web.

Topic: Colonial America

Definition/Introduction

- ### *What is the topic? What does it cover?*

  The colonial period in American history lasted from the settlement at Jamestown in 1607 through the American Revolutionary War in 1775. This was a time of growth and the development of an identity for the new country.

- ### *Catalog Subject Headings or Keywords*

  United States history 1600-1775, Colonial period
  Pilgrims (New England colonists)
  Puritans
  Plymouth
  Williamsburg (VA)

- ### *Dewey Numbers*

  973.2 United States history, Colonial period

Print Resources

- ### *Reference titles [dictionaries, encyclopedias, atlases, specific subject references]*

  American Historical Images on File. Facts On File, c1990-c1991.

  Colonial America. UXL, c2000.

  King, David C. *First Facts About American Heroes.* Blackbirch Press, c1996.

  North America in Colonial Times: An Encyclopedia For Students. Charles Scribner's Sons , Simon & Schuster and Prentice Hall International, c1998.

  Purvis, Thomas L. *Colonial America to 1763.* Facts On File, c1999.

- ### *General titles [nonfiction, any suitable fiction]*

  Be sure to check the library online catalog to find additional suitable materials.

  Brown, Gene. *Discovery and Settlement: Europe Meets the New World, 1490-1700.* Twenty-First Century Books, c1993.

  Day, Nancy. *Your Travel Guide To Colonial America.* Runestone, c2001.

  Edwards, Judith. *Jamestown, John Smith, and Pocahontas In American History.* Enslow Publishers, c2002.

Egger-Bovet, Howard. *Uskids History. Book of the American Colonies*. Little, Brown, c1996.

Furbee, Mary R. *Outrageous Women of Colonial America*. John Wiley, c2001.

Steins, Richard. *Colonial America*. Raintree Steck-Vaughn, c2000.

■ *Journals*

Be sure to check any online periodical database at your school library for more.

Beaumont, Stephen; Forman, Janet. "Liberty Inn". *American Heritage,* Jun2003, Vol. 54 Issue 3, p26, 8p, 6c

"Colonial Kids". *Kids Discover*, Nov93, Vol. 3 Issue 9, p12, 2p, 1 cartoon, 8c, 2bw

"The People Who Made Colonial America". *Scholastic News—Senior Edition*, 12/13/99 Map Skills Practice, Vol. 68 Issue 12, p4, 2p, 1 diagram

"What, Where, When, And Who Was Colonial America?" *Kids Discover*, Nov93, Vol. 3 Issue 9, p4, 2p, 8c

Web Resources

Archiving Early America
http://earlyamerica.com/
"Scenes and portraits from original newspapers, maps and writings come to life on your screen just as they appeared to this country's forebears more than two centuries ago."

Colonial Hall
http://www.colonialhall.com/
Biographies of our founding fathers.

Colonial North America
http://www.fordham.edu/halsall/mod/modsbook07.html
Information about Colonial America from the early conquest and exploration.

Colonial Williamsburg
http://www.history.org/
Information about the founding of Williamsburg and the living museum.

Plimoth Plantation
http://www.plimoth.org/
Take a virtual tour of this living museum.

Virtual Jamestown
http://www.virtualjamestown.org/page2.html
Information about the settlement at Jamestown including first-hand accounts and letters.

Topic: American Revolution

Middle School Library Pathfinder

Pathfinders are guides which are intended to help you get started doing research on a particular topic, both online and at your library. Although these resources are useful as a starting point for your research, they are not the only resources that are available to you.

Definition/Introduction

■ *What is the topic? What does it cover?*

During the latter part of the 18th century, the settlers in America grew more and more unsatisfied with being governed by the British. As more and more Americans began to talk about independence, the idea grew until there was only one thing they could do. In 1775, they declared their independence and began a long battle to establish their right to form a new country.

■ *Catalog Subject Headings or Keywords*

United States history 1775-1783
Revolution
Revolutionary War
American Revolution

■ *Dewey Numbers*

973.3 General United States history—Revolution

Print Resources

■ *Reference titles [dictionaries, encyclopedias, atlases, specific subject references]*

American Revolution. UXL, c2000.

Encyclopedia of American History. Facts On File, c2003.

English, June A. *Scholastic Encyclopedia of the United States at War.* Scholastic Reference, c1998.

Purvis, Thomas L. *Revolutionary America, 1763 to 1800.* Facts On File, c1995.

Reef, Catherine. *African Americans in the Military.* Facts On File, c2004.

■ *General titles [nonfiction, any suitable fiction]*

Be sure to check the library online catalog to find additional suitable materials.

American Revolution: Battles and Leaders. DK Publishing, c2004.

Bolden, Tonya. *American Patriots: The Story of Blacks in the Military From the Revolution to Desert Storm.* Crown Publishers, c2003.

Green, Carl R. *The Revolutionary War.* MyReportLinks.com Books, c2002.

Maynard, Christopher. *The History News: Revolution.* Candlewick Press, c1999.

McGowen, Tom. *The Revolutionary War and George Washington's Army in American History.* Enslow Publishers, c2004.

Slavicek, Louise Chipley. *Women of the American Revolution*. Lucent Books, Thomson/Gale, c2003.

Stewart, Gail. *Life of a Soldier in Washington's Army*. Lucent Books, Thomson/Gale, c2003.

■ *Journals*

Be sure to check any online periodical database at your school library for more.

Caes, Charles J. "Midnight Riders". (cover story) American History, Dec2004, Vol. 39 Issue 5, p34, 8p, 6c, 2bw

Currie, Stephen. "A Difficult Decade". Cobblestone, Dec2004, Vol. 25 Issue 9, p2, 4p, 3c

Ellis, Joseph. "Inventing: The Presidency". American Heritage, Oct2004, Vol. 55 Issue 5, p43, 9p, 1 map, 5c, 2bw

Ellis, Joseph J. "Washington Takes Charge". Smithsonian, Jan2005, Vol. 35 Issue 10, p92, 10p, 8c, 4bw

Ferling, John. "The Rocky Road to Revolution". Smithsonian, Jul2004, Vol. 35 Issue 4, p96, 10p, 13c, 2bw

"Waves of Immigration". Scholastic News—Senior Edition, 12/13/99 Map Skills Practice, Vol. 68 Issue 12, p10, 2p, 1bw

Web Resources

American Revolution Home Page
http://www.americanrevwar.homestead.com/files/INDEX2.HTM
From the prelude to the War through the aftermath, this site has it all.

America's Freedom Documents
http://www.earlyamerica.com/freedom/index.html
Here are the "Freedom Documents" from Early America—the Declaration of Independence, the Constitution, and the Bill of Rights.

The History Place
http://www.historyplace.com/unitedstates/revolution/index.html
Information about the beginnings of America from the early explorations and colonial era through the birth of the nation.

Liberty! The American Revolution
http://www.pbs.org/ktca/liberty/
From the PBS show, gives information about events leading to the war as well as the people involved.

Topic: U. S. Constitution

Definition/Introduction

■ *What is the topic? What does it cover?*

When the American colonists won the Revolutionary War, they won the right and responsibility to govern their new country. The Founding Fathers knew that the new government needed a set of rules. To define the rules for the new government, they created a document called the Constitution.

■ *Catalog Subject Headings or Keywords*

Constitution
Bill of Rights
Amendments
Constitutional Convention
Continental Congress
> *See also specific amendments and names of signers of the Constitution*

■ *Dewey Numbers*

323.4 Freedom of Assembly, Freedom of Religion, Freedom of Press, Freedom of Speech
342.73 United States Constitution
973.3 United States Constitutional History

Print Resources

■ *Reference titles [dictionaries, encyclopedias, atlases, specific subject references]*

Encyclopedia of the American Constitution. Macmillan Reference USA, c2000.

Feinberg, Barbara Silberdick. *The Dictionary of the U.S. Constitution.* Franklin Watts, c1999.

Maddex, Robert L. *The U.S. Constitution A to Z.* CQ Press, c2002.

Pendergast, Tom. *Constitutional Amendments: From Freedom of Speech to Flag Burning.* UXL, c2001.

Vile, John R. *Encyclopedia of Constitutional Amendments, Proposed Amendments, and Amending Issues, 1789-2002.* ABC-CLIO, c2003.

■ *General titles [nonfiction, any suitable fiction]*

Be sure to check the library online catalog to find additional suitable materials.

Collier, Christopher. *Creating the Constitution, 1787*. Benchmark Books, c1999.

Freedman, Russell. *In Defense of Liberty: The Story of America's Bill of Rights*. Holiday House, c2003.

Horn, Geoffrey M. *The Bill of Rights and Other Amendments*. World Almanac Library, c2004.

Marcovitz, Hal. *The Constitution*. Mason Crest Publishers, c2003.

Quinn, C. Edward. *The Signers of the Constitution of the United States*. Grolier Educational, 1996.

Sherman, Josepha. *The Constitution*. Rosen Pub. Group, c2004.

■ *Journals*

Be sure to check any online periodical database at your school library for more.

Alter, Jonathan. "Your Right to Know Is at Stake". *Newsweek*, 2/28/2005, Vol. 145 Issue 9, p36, 1p, 1c

"My So-called Rights". (cover story) *Scholastic Update*, 11/3/95, Vol. 128 Issue 5, p4, 2p, 5c

Weisberger, Bernard A. "Amending America". *American Heritage*, May/Jun95, Vol. 46 Issue 3, p24, 2p, 1bw

Web Resources

Ben's Guide to Government for Kids
http://bensguide.gpo.gov/6-8/documents/index.html
Explains historical documents including the Declaration of Independence, The Constitution, the Bill of Rights, and others.

The PBS Kids Democracy Project: How Does Government Affect Me?
http://pbskids.org/democracy/mygovt/capitol1.html
This site has clear explanations of the three branches of government set up by the Constitution. You can also find out about what it's like to be president of the U.S. for a day and why voting is important.

To Form a More Perfect Union
http://lcweb2.loc.gov/ammem/bdsds/bdexhome.html
Site contains information about the work of the Continental Congress and the Constitutional Convention.

Topic: Lewis and Clark Expedition

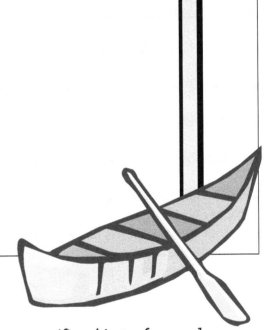

Definition/Introduction

■ *What is the topic? What does it cover?*

In 1804, Captain Meriwether Lewis and Captain William Clark set out to find out if they could travel overland to the Pacific Ocean following the Missouri and Columbia Rivers. They eventually reached the Pacific Ocean in 1805.

■ *Catalog Subject Headings or Keywords*

Lewis and Clark Expedition
Lewis, Meriwether
Clark, William
Corps of Discovery
Sacagawea
Explorers

■ *Dewey Numbers*

917   Geography and travel – North America
973.4 Lewis and Clark Expedition (1804-1805)
978   West (US) – Expeditions
979.5 Pacific Northeast

Print Resources

■ *Reference titles [dictionaries, encyclopedias, atlases, specific subject references]*

Encyclopedia of the American Constitution. Macmillan Reference USA, c2000.

Hakim, Joy. *The New Nation.* Oxford University Press, c2003.

Profiles in American History. Volume 2, Constitutional Convention to the War of 1812. UXL, c1994.

Woodger, Elin. *Encyclopedia of the Lewis and Clark Expedition.* Facts On File, c2004.

■ *General titles [nonfiction, any suitable fiction]*

Be sure to check the library online catalog to find additional suitable materials.

Cavan, Seamus. *Lewis and Clark and the Route to the Pacific.* Chelsea House, c1991.

Edwards, Judith. *Lewis and Clark's Journey of Discovery in American History.* Enslow Publishers, c1999.

Isaacs, Sally Senzell. *The Lewis and Clark Expedition.* Heinemann Library, c2004.

Marcovitz, Hal. *Sacagawea: Guide For the Lewis and Clark Expedition*. Chelsea House, c2001.

Santella, Andrew. *Lewis and Clark*. Franklin Watts, c2001.

■ *Journals*

Be sure to check any online periodical database at your school library for more.

Brandt, Anthony. "The Perilous Afterlife of the Lewis and Clark Expedition". *American Heritage*, Jul2004, Vol. 55 Issue 3, p50, 8p, 1 map, 5c

"The Missouri Breaks". *Smithsonian*, Mar2005, Vol. 35 Issue 12, p28, 1p, 1c

Winchester, Elizabeth. "Remembering Lewis & Clark". *Time for Kids*, 5/7/2004 World Edition, Vol. 9 Issue 26, p6, 1p, 1 map, 4c

Web Resources

Discovering Lewis and Clark

http://www.lewis-clark.org/

"Focuses on issues, values and visions relating to the Lewis & Clark Expedition, its preludes, and its aftermath up to the present time."

Echoes of a Bitter Crossing: Lewis and Clark in Idaho

http://idptv.state.id.us/lc/

Visit this site to find out the Native American contributions to this difficult part of the journey.

Journey of the Corps of Discovery

http://www.pbs.org/lewisandclark/

Produced to accompany the PBS film, this site has in-depth information about the people and events of the expedition. Includes lots of information about the interactions with Native Americans during the expedition.

Lewis and Clark—Mapping the West

http://www2.edgate.com/lewisandclark/

This site from the Smithsonian Institute provides kid-friendly information about the journey, along with lesson plans and activities for learning about mapmaking.

Lewis and Clark at National Geographic

http://www.nationalgeographic.com/lewisclark/index.html

Join the Lewis and Clark expedition in this interactive journey based on the book *How We Crossed the West: The Adventures of Lewis and Clark* by Rosalyn Schanzer.

Topic: Underground Railroad

Definition/Introduction

■ *What is the topic? What does it cover?*

The Underground Railroad was a network of safe houses and other places established on the route to the North before the Civil War. These places provided sanctuary and assistance to escaped slaves seeking to be free.

■ *Catalog Subject Headings or Keywords*

Underground Railroad
Slavery
Antislavery movements
Civil War
Emancipation

■ *Dewey Numbers*

326 Slavery and emancipation
973.6 United States history, 1845-1861

Print Resources

■ *Reference titles [dictionaries, encyclopedias, atlases, specific subject references]*

Klein, Martin A. *The A to Z of Slavery and Abolition.* Scarecrow Press, c2002.
Slavery Throughout History. UXL, c2000.
Student Almanac of African American History. Greenwood Press, c2003.

■ *General titles [nonfiction, any suitable fiction]*

Be sure to check the library online catalog to find additional suitable materials.
Fradin, Dennis B. *Bound for the North Star: True Stories of Fugitive Slaves.* Clarion Books, c2000.
Haskins, James. *Get On Board: The Story of the Underground Railroad.* Scholastic, c1993.
Issacs, Sally Senzell. *Life on the Underground Railroad.* Heinemann Library, c2002.
Lester, Julius. *To Be a Slave.* Dial Books, c1998.
Sawyer, Kem Knapp. *The Underground Railroad in American History.* Enslow Publishers, c1997.
Swain, Gwenyth. *President of the Underground Railroad: A Story About Levi Coffin.* Carolrhoda Books, c2001.

■ *Journals*

Be sure to check any online periodical database at your school library for more.

"The Antislavery Movement", *Cobblestone Magazine*, February 1993, Vol. 14, Issue 2

Crew, Spencer R. "All Aboard the Underground Railroad". *Cobblestone*, Feb2003, Vol. 24 Issue 2, p3, 4p, 4c

Sharif, Dara N. "Freedom's Trail". *Scholastic News—Senior Edition*, 1/17/2003, Vol. 71 Issue 14, p4, 2p, 3c, 2bw

Wellington, Darryl Lorenzo. "The Most Famous Abductor On The Underground Railroad". *Christian Science Monitor*, 1/20/2004, Vol. 96 Issue 37, p19, 0p, 1c

Web Resources

Aboard the Underground Railroad: A National Register Travel Itinerary
http://www.cr.nps.gov/nr/travel/underground
Description of the houses connected with the Underground Railroad, including the Nathan and Polly Johnson house on 7th Street.

National Underground Railroad Freedom Center
http://www.freedomcenter.org
Learn about the Underground Railroad and the struggle for freedom.

Underground Railroad
http://www.pbs.org/wgbh/aia/part4/4p2944.html
The Underground Railroad, a vast network of people who helped fugitive slaves escape to the North and to Canada, was not run by any single organization or person. Rather, it consisted of many individuals—many whites but predominantly black—who knew only of the local efforts to aid fugitives and not of the overall operation. Still, it effectively moved hundreds of slaves northward each year—according to one estimate, the South lost 100,000 slaves between 1810 and 1850.

Underground Railroad Routes 1860
http://education.ucdavis.edu/NEW/STC/lesson/socstud/railroad/Map.htm
The Underground Railroad was a loose association of people, not a system of tracks. Indeed, much of a typical flight to freedom involved many miles of walking, usually at night to avoid detection. Still, it is possible to see these patterns in the escape routes. The refugee slaves tended to areas of easier, known, and more secretive routes, such as the Mississippi River and the Appalachian Mountains.

A Virtual Tour of the Underground Railroad: You Are an Escaped Slave. How will you survive?
http://www.nationalgeographic.com/features/99/railroad/
Imagine you are a slave in the 1850s. You've never known freedom but you are about to begin a hard, dangerous journey to find it.

Topic: Civil War

Definition/Introduction

- ### *What is the topic? What does it cover?*

  The Civil War was fought from 1861 to 1865. The Southern or Confederate States believed that the individual states should have more rights. The Northern or Union States fought to keep the country together.

- ### *Catalog Subject Headings or Keywords*

  United States history 1861-1865
  Civil War
  War Between the States
  War of Secession
  > *See also names of individuals associated with the war and names of individual battles.*

- ### *Dewey Numbers*

  973.7 Civil War

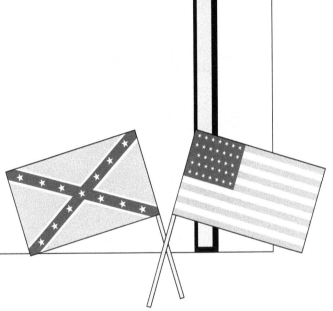

Print Resources

- ### *Reference titles [dictionaries, encyclopedias, atlases, specific subject references]*

  Civil War. UXL, c2000.

  American Eras. Civil War and Reconstruction, 1850-1877. Gale Research, c1997.

  The Atlas of the Civil War. Courage, c2005.

  Bolotin, Norm. *Civil War A To Z: A Young Readers' Guide to Over 100 People, Places, and Points of Importance.* Dutton Children's Books, c2002.

  Netzley, Patricia D. *The Greenhaven Encyclopedia of the Civil War.* Greenhaven Press, Thomson/Gale, c2004.

  Seldman, Rachel Filene. *The Civil War: A History In Documents.* Oxford University Press, c2001.

- ### *General titles [nonfiction, any suitable fiction]*

  Be sure to check the library online catalog to find additional suitable materials.

  Beller, Susan Provost. *The Civil War.* Benchmark Books, c2003.

  Collier, Christopher. *The Civil War, 1860-1865.* Benchmark Books, c2000.

  Day, Nancy. *Your Travel Guide to Civil War America.* Runestone, c2001.

  Grant, R. G. *The African-American Slave Trade.* Barron's, 2003.

Green, Carl R. *Confederate Generals Of The Civil War.* Enslow Publishers, c1998.

Kent, Zachary. *The Civil War: "A House Divided".* Enslow Publishers, c1994.

Murphy, Jim. *The Long Road to Gettysburg.* Clarion Books, c1992.

Profiles in American History. UXL, c1994.

■ Journals

Be sure to check any online periodical database at your school library for more.

Harper, Judith E. "Volunteers for the Blue and the Gray". *Cobblestone*, Feb2005, Vol. 26 Issue 2, p18, 3p, 4bw

Lees, William B. "A Clash of Cultures". *dig*, Feb2004, Vol. 6 Issue 2, p16, 4p

Youhn, Susan. "Angels of the Battlefield". *Cobblestone*, Feb2005, Vol. 26 Issue 2, p8, 6p, 3c, 2bw

Web Resources

American Civil War Collections at the Electronic Text Center
http://etext.virginia.edu/civilwar/
Home to a variety of primary source material on the American Civil War, including letters, diaries, and newspapers.

American Civil War Homepage
http://sunsite.utk.edu/civil-war/
"The *American Civil War Homepage* gathers together in one place hypertext links to the most useful identified electronic files about the American Civil War (1861-1865)."

Civil War Maps
http://lcweb2.loc.gov/ammem/collections/civil_war_maps/
Civil War Maps brings together materials from three premier collections: the Library of Congress Geography and Map Division, the Virginia Historical Society, and the Library of Virginia.

Kidport Reference Library
http://kidport.com/RefLib/UsaHistory/CivilWar/CivilWar.htm
Kidport pages on the Civil War include links to other pages and a timeline of the war.

Selected Civil War Photographs
http://memory.loc.gov/ammem/cwphtml/cwphome.html
The Selected Civil War Photographs Collection contains 1,118 photographs. Most of the images were made under the supervision of Mathew B. Brady, and include scenes of military personnel, preparations for battle, and battle after-effects. The collection also includes portraits of both Confederate and Union officers, and a selection of enlisted men.

The United States Civil War Center
http://www.cwc.lsu.edu/cwc/civlink.htm
Links to many pages about all aspects of the Civil War.

Topic: Westward Expansion

Middle School Library Pathfinder

Pathfinders are guides which are intended to help you get started doing research on a particular topic, both online and at your library. Although these resources are useful as a starting point for your research, they are not the only resources that are available to you.

Definition/Introduction

■ *What is the topic? What does it cover?*

For many years, the land west of the Mississippi was not a common destination for settlers. After 1850, this changed dramatically. The gold strike in California, the Homestead Act of 1862, and the pioneering spirit led to the opening of the west and the westward expansion.

■ *Catalog Subject Headings or Keywords*

Westward expansion
Frontier and pioneer life
Oregon Trail
West (U.S.)
> *See also individuals associated with this time period and names of individual states and territories.*

■ *Dewey Numbers*

978   West (U.S.)

Print Resources

■ *Reference titles [dictionaries, encyclopedias, atlases, specific subject references]*

American Eras. Westward Expansion, 1800-1860. Gale Research, c1999.

Profiles in American History. Volume 4, Westward Movement to the Civil War. UXL, c1994.

Westward Expansion. UXL, c2000, c2001.

■ *General titles [nonfiction, any suitable fiction]*

Be sure to check the library online catalog to find additional suitable materials.

Isaacs, Sally Senzell. *America in the Time of Lewis and Clark, 1801-1850.* Heinemann Library, c1998.

King, David C. *Westward Expansion.* John Wiley, c2003.

Nelson, Sheila. *From Sea to Shining Sea: Americans Move West 1846-1860.* Mason Crest Publishers, c2005.

Olsen, Steven P. *The Oregon Trail: A Primary Source History of the Route to the American West.* Rosen Central, c2004.

Steele, Christy. *Famous Wagon Trails.* World Almanac Library, c2005.

Steele, Christy. *Pioneer Life in the American West*. World Almanac Library, c2005.

Stefoff, Rebecca. *The Opening of the West*. Benchmark Books, c2003.

Wittmann, Kelly. *Explorers of the American West*. Mason Crest Publishers, c2003.

■ *Journals*

Be sure to check any online periodical database at your school library for more.

"Donner Party". *American History & Politics*, 1850-1914, 2002, p5, 3p

"Frontier America". *American History & Politics*, 1607-1849, 2002, p21, 2p

"Heading West". (cover story) *Economist*, 12/31/99, Vol. 353 Issue 8151, Millennium issue p48, 3p, 1 map

Web Resources

American Experience - Gold Rush!
http://pbskids.org/wayback/goldrush/
Explore summer vacations of the past, flight, the California Gold Rush, the women's and civil rights movements, and technology in 1900. From the PBS show American Experience.

Life of Sacagawea
http://www.usmint.gov/mint_programs/golden_dollar_coin/index.cfm?flash=yes&action=about_sacagawea
Biography from the United States Mint.

National Park Service Trail of Tears
http://www.nps.gov/trte/
The Trail of Tears National Historic Trail commemorates the removal of the Cherokee and the paths that 17 Cherokee detachments followed westward.

The Oregon Trail
http://www.isu.edu/~trinmich/Oregontrail.html
This web site is brought to you by teachers Mike Trinklein and Steve Boettcher, creators of The Oregon Trail, the award-winning documentary film that aired on PBS.

Virtual Museum of the City of San Francisco
http://www.sfmuseum.org/hist1/rail.html
Driving the Last Spike. Information about the railroad to the West.

WestWeb
http://www.library.csi.cuny.edu/westweb/
WestWeb is a topically organized Web site about the study of the American West.

Topic: Child Labor During the Industrial Revolution

Definition/Introduction

- ### What is the topic? What does it cover?

The Industrial Revolution was a time of dramatic change, from hand tools and handmade items, to products that were mass-produced by machines. Workers became more productive, and since more items were manufactured, prices dropped, making exclusive and hard-to-make items available to the poor and not only to the rich and elite. Life generally improved, but the Industrial Revolution also proved harmful. Pollution increased, working conditions were dangerous, and capitalists employed women and young children, making them work long and hard hours. The Industrial Revolution was a time of change—for the better, or for the worse.

- ### Catalog Subject Headings or Keywords

Industrial Revolution
[name of country] – Economic conditions
Industries – History
Child labor
Children – Employment
Factories

- ### Dewey Numbers

330.9 Economic situation and conditions
909.81 History of 19th century

Print Resources

- ### Reference titles [dictionaries, encyclopedias, atlases, specific subject references]

Encyclopedia of American History. Facts On File, c2003.

Olson, James Stuart. *Encyclopedia of the Industrial Revolution in America*. Greenwood Press, c2002.

Outman, James L. *Industrial Revolution*. Thomson/Gale, c2003.

- ## *General titles [nonfiction, any suitable fiction]*

  Be sure to check the library online catalog to find additional suitable materials.

  Bartoletti, Susan Campbell. *Kids On Strike!* Houghton Mifflin, c1999.

  Child Labor in America. Discovery Enterprises, c1997.

  Connolly, Sean. *The Industrial Revolution.* Heinemann Library, c2003.

  Freedman, Russell. *Kids At Work: Lewis Hine and the Crusade Against Child Labor.* Clarion Books, c1994.

- ## *Journals*

  Be sure to check any online periodical database at your school library for more.

  "Industrial Revolution". *CQ Researcher*, 8/31/2001, Vol. 11 Issue 29, p670, 4p, 1 chart

  "The March of Industry". *Kids Discover*, Nov2001, Vol. 11 Issue 11, p4, 2p, 16

  "Permanent Revolution". *Kids Discover*, Nov2001, Vol. 11 Issue 11, p16, 2p, 5c

Web Resources

Camella Teoli Testifies about the 1912 Lawrence Textile Strike
http://historymatters.gmu.edu/d/61/
Fourteen-year-old Camella Teoli delivered testimony before the U.S. Congressional hearings about the working conditions in the Lawrence Textile mill.

Child Labor in Factories
http://nhs.needham.k12.ma.us/cur/Baker_00/2002_p7/ak_p7/childlabor.html
Information about child workers during the Industrial Revolution.

Eyewitness at the Triangle
http://www.ilr.cornell.edu/trianglefire/texts/stein_ootss/ootss_wgs.html?location=Fire!
The nation learned of the horrible fire at the Triangle Shirtwaist Company. This document first appeared in the Milwaukee Journal, March 27, 1911.

The History Place: Child Labor in America 1908-1912
http://www.historyplace.com/unitedstates/childlabor/
Photographs taken by Lewis W. Hine.

Twenty Years at Hull-House by Jane Addams
http://digital.library.upenn.edu/women/addams/hullhouse/hullhouse.html
Presents Hull House founder Jane Addams' account of her work at the settlement home in Chicago's West side slums during the years between 1889 to 1909.

The Urban Log Cabin
http://www.thirteen.org/tenement/logcabin.html
Come along for a virtual visit to the tenements that more than 10,000 people called home between the years 1870 and 1915.

Topic: Great Depression

Definition/Introduction

■ What is the topic? What does it cover?

The stock market crash of 1929 resulted from millions of dollars being wiped off the United States stock values. People who had invested their life savings in the stock market suddenly had nothing. And since many people invested money they did not really have, they lost everything. This began years of economic depression.

■ Catalog Subject Headings or Keywords

New Deal
Depressions, 1929
United States – History
Dust Bowl
Migrant workers
Great Depression

■ Dewey Numbers

338.5 General production economics
973.91 U.S. history 1901-1953

Brother Can You Spare a Dime?

Print Resources

■ Reference titles [dictionaries, encyclopedias, atlases, specific subject references]

American Decades.1930-1939: Primary Sources. Gale, Thomson/Gale, c2004.

Encyclopedia of American History. Facts On File, c2003.

The *Great Depression*. Thomson/Gale, c2002.

Hanes, Sharon M. *The Great Depression and New Deal Reference Library*. UXL, Thomson/Gale, c2003.

Profiles in American History. Volume 7, Great Depression to the Cuban Missile Crisis. UXL, c1995.

■ General titles [nonfiction, any suitable fiction]

Be sure to check the library online catalog to find additional suitable materials.

Burgan, Michael. *The Great Depression*. Compass Point Books, c2002.

Fremon, David K. *The Great Depression in American History*. Enslow Publishers, c1997.

Gow, Mary. *The Stock Market Crash of 1929: Dawn of the Great Depression*. Enslow Publishers, c2003.

Profiles in American History. UXL, c1994.

Ruggiero, Adriane. *The Great Depression.* Benchmark Books, c2005.

Wroble, Lisa A. *The New Deal and the Great Depression in American History.* Enslow, c2002.

■ Journals

Be sure to check any online periodical database at your school library for more.

Garraty, John A. "The Big Picture of the Great Depression". *American Heritage*, Aug/Sep86, Vol. 37 Issue 5, p90, 8p, 5bw

"The Great Depression". (cover story) *Maclean's*, 07/01/99, Vol. 112 Issue 26, p48, 2p, 2bw

Lord, Lewis. "The Week that 'Saved Capitalism'" *U.S. News & World Report*, 3/31/2003, Vol. 134 Issue 10, p2, 1p, 2bw

Lord, Lewis. "A Winter that 'Chilled Like the World's End'". *U.S. News & World Report*, 1/20/2003, Vol. 134 Issue 2, p12, 1p, 4c

Samuleson, Robert J. "What We Learn From the 1920s". *Newsweek*, 02/12/2001, Vol. 137 Issue 7, p33, 1p, 1c

Ward, Geoffrey C. "1932 A New Deal Is Struck". *Smithsonian*, Oct2004, Vol. 35 Issue 7, p60, 3p, 1c, 10bw

Web Resources

The New Deal Network
http://newdeal.feri.org/
Includes classroom activities and Internet projects. It is sponsored by the Franklin and Eleanor Roosevelt Institute.

Library of Congress site for "Voices from the Dust Bowl"
http://lcweb2.loc.gov/ammem/afctshtml/tshome.html
Part of the American Memory project.

New Deal Cultural Programs
http://www.wwcd.org/policy/US/newdeal.html
Written by Don Adams and Arlene Goldbard. Explains the federal cultural programs created during the New Deal.

Topic: World War I

Middle School Library Pathfinder

Pathfinders are guides which are intended to help you get started doing research on a particular topic, both online and at your library. Although these resources are useful as a starting point for your research, they are not the only resources that are available to you.

Definition/Introduction

■ *What is the topic? What does it cover?*

World War I was fought between the Central European Powers (Germany, Austria-Hungary, and the Allies) on one side and the Triple-Entente (Britain, France, Russia, and later, the United States) on the other side. The war lasted from 1914-1918.

■ *Catalog Subject Headings or Keywords*

World War, 1914-1918
European War
  See also individuals associated with the war, and individual battles and countries.

■ *Dewey Numbers*

940.3 World War I
940.4 Military history of World War I

Print Resources

■ *Reference titles [dictionaries, encyclopedias, atlases, specific subject references]*

Encyclopedia of World War I (Five Volume Set) ABC-CLIO, c2005.

Pendergast, Tom. *World War I Reference Library.* UXL, Gale Group/Thomson Learning, c2002.

Pendergast, Tom. *World War I. Almanac.* UXL, Gale Group/Thomson Learning, c2002.

Pendergast, Tom. *World War I. Biographies.* UXL, c2002.

Pendergast, Tom. *World War I. Primary Sources.* UXL, Gale Group/Thomson Learning, c2002.

■ *General titles [nonfiction, any suitable fiction]*

Be sure to check the library online catalog to find additional suitable materials.

Feldman, Ruth Tenzer. *World War I.* Lerner Publications, c2004.

George, Linda S. *World War I.* Benchmark Books, c2002.

Grant, R.G. *Armistice 1918.* Raintree Steck-Vaughn, c2001.

Hamilton, John. *Battles of World War I.* Abdo, c2004.

Kent, Zachary. *World War I: "The War To End Wars".* Enslow Publishers, c1994.

Ross, Stewart. *Leaders of World War I.* Raintree Steck-Vaughn, c2003.

Web Resources

Art of the First World War
http://www.art-ww1.com/gb/index2.html

An exhibition of 110 paintings brought together by the major history museums of Europe. World War I as seen by 54 painters on both sides.

Encyclopaedia of the First World War
http://www.spartacus.schoolnet.co.uk/FWW.htm

A wealth of information about the war. It is organized by various topics including technology, art, and literature.

The Great War and the Shaping of the 20th Century
http://www.pbs.org/greatwar/

The companion Web site for "The Great War and the Shaping of the 20th Century,"KCET/BBC co-production in association with The Imperial War Museum.

Navsource-World War I Special Feature—Mike Corwith Photo Collection
http://www.navsource.org/archives/features/corwith/corwith2.htm

Images of the naval scenes during World War I.

World War I Document Archive
http://www.lib.byu.edu/~rdh/wwi/

This archive of primary documents from World War I has been assembled by volunteers of the World War I Military History List (WWI-L).

World War I Photos of the Great War
http://www.gwpda.org/photos/greatwar.htm

These are the images of that time, an eternal testament to all those whose lives were lost or forever altered by "The Great War."

World War I Posters
http://afsf.lackland.af.mil/Images/WWI/

A gallery of World War I posters from the United States Armed Forces Security forces Web site.

Topic: World War II

Definition/Introduction

■ *What is the topic? What does it cover?*

World War II was fought from 1939-1945. The war was between Germany, Italy, and Japan (the Axis powers) on one side and Britain, France, the United States, the USSR, and China (the Allied powers) on the other.

■ *Catalog Subject Headings or Keywords*

World War, 1939-1945
World War II
    See also names of persons, battles, campaigns, sieges, etc.

■ *Dewey Numbers*

940.53 World War II
940.54 Military history of World War II

Print Resources

■ *Reference titles [dictionaries, encyclopedias, atlases, specific subject references]*

American Home Front in World War II. UXL, Thomson/Gale, c2005.

Encyclopedia of World War II: A Political, Social, and Military History. ABC-CLIO, c2005.

Feldman, George. *World War II: Almanac.* UXL, 1999

World War II A Student Encyclopedia. (5 Volume Set) ABC-CLIO, c2005.

■ *General titles [nonfiction, any suitable fiction]*

Be sure to check the library online catalog to find additional suitable materials.

Gonzales, Doreen. *The Manhattan Project and the Atomic Bomb in American History.* Enslow Publishers, c2000.

Holocaust Memories: Speaking the Truth. Franklin Watts, c2001.

Lawton, Clive. *Hiroshima: The Story of the First Atom Bomb.* Candlewick Press, c2004.

Ruggiero, Adriane. *World War II.* Benchmark Books, c2003.

■ *Journals*

Be sure to check any online periodical database at your school library for more.

Anderson, Christopher J. "Ordinary Men Achieving Extraordinary Things". *American History*, Aug2004, Vol. 39 Issue 3, p40, 7p, 3c, 2bw

Spiller, Roger J. "World War II 1941 to 1945". *American Heritage*, Nov/Dec2004, Vol. 55 Issue 6, p56, 3p, 1c

"World War II Letters Home" *Junior Scholastic*, 4/25/2003, Vol. 105 Issue 17, p12, 2p, 2c

Web Resources

American Memory: From the Depression to World War II
http://memory.loc.gov/ammem/fsowhome.html
The Library of Congress presents these documents as part of the record of the past. These primary historical documents reflect the attitudes, perspectives, and beliefs of different times.

The History Place: World War Two in Europe
http://www.historyplace.com/worldwar2/
A timeline of World War II and the Holocaust.

A People at War
http://www.archives.gov/exhibit_hall/a_people_at_war/a_people_at_war.html
The National Archives and Records Administration highlights the contributions of thousands Americans who served during WWII.

World War II Commemoration
http://www.archives.gov/exhibit_hall/a_people_at_war/a_people_at_war.html
Grolier created this commemorative for the 50th anniversary of the end of the war.

WWII Resources
http://www.ibiblio.org/pha/
One of the best places for primary resources related to the war that is broken down into categories.

World War II Document
http://www.ibiblio.org/pha/
World War II documents compiled by The Avalon Project at Yale Law School.

Evacuation and Internment of San Francisco Japanese
http://www.sfmuseum.org/war/evactxt.html
The Virtual Museum of San Francisco provides this site that provides a chronological listing and links to information about the internment.

Topic: Civil Rights Movement

Definition/Introduction

- ### *What is the topic? What does it cover?*

  For much of the time following the Civil War, African Americans were not treated equally. They were not allowed to go to the same schools, eat in the same restaurants, or have the same career opportunities as others. During the 1950s, a concerted struggle to obtain civil rights came into the spotlight.

- ### *Catalog Subject Headings or Keywords*

  Civil rights
  Civil disobedience
  Boycott
  Voting rights
  Freedom riders
  Segregation
  Desegregation
  Integration
  Sit-ins

- ### *Dewey Numbers*

  322   Organized groups
  323   Civil and political rights
  973.9   United State history, 1901-
      See also individual biographies.

Middle School Library Pathfinder

Pathfinders are guides which are intended to help you get started doing research on a particular topic, both online and at your library. Although these resources are useful as a starting point for your research, they are not the only resources that are available to you.

Print Resources

- ### *Reference titles [dictionaries, encyclopedias, atlases, specific subject references]*

  African American Biography. UXL, c1994.

  American Lives. Oxford University Press, c2004.

  American Civil Rights. Primary Sources. UXL, c1999.

  Civil Rights in the United States. Macmillan Reference USA, c2000.

  Engelbert, Phillis. *American Civil Rights. Biographies.* UXL, c1999.

■ *General titles [nonfiction, any suitable fiction]*

Be sure to check the library online catalog to find additional suitable materials.

Dunn, John M. *The Civil Rights Movement.* Lucent Books, c1998.

Finlayson, Reggie. *We Shall Overcome: The History of the American Civil Rights Movement.* Lerner Publications, c2003.

McWhorter, Diane. *A Dream of Freedom: The Civil Rights Movement From 1954 to 1968.* Scholastic Nonfiction, c2004.

Patterson, Charles. *The Civil Rights Movement.* Facts On File, c1995.

Profiles In American History. UXL, c1994.

Somerlott, Robert. *The Little Rock School Desegregation Crisis in American History.* Enslow Publishers, c2001.

■ *Journals*

Be sure to check any online periodical database at your school library for more.

Butler, Carolyn Kleiner. "Down in Mississippi". *Smithsonian*, Feb2005, Vol. 35 Issue 11, p23, 2p, 1c, 1bw

Kulman, Linda. "The Power of a Moment". (cover story) *U.S. News & World Report*, 3/22/2004, Vol. 136 Issue 10, p95, 1p, 1c

Schindehette, Susan; Stolley, Richard B.; Harmel, Kristin. "Justice for All". *People*, 5/17/2004, Vol. 61 Issue 19, p56, 4p, 4c, 5bw

Web Resources

The Civil Rights Era
http://memory.loc.gov/ammem/aaohtml/exhibit/aopart9.html
From the African American Odyssey.

The Civil Rights Movement
http://www.cnn.com/EVENTS/1997/mlk/links.html%20
Timeline of the civil rights movement.

The History of Jim Crow
http://www.jimcrowhistory.org/home.htm
Explore the complex African-American experience of segregation from the 1870s through the 1950s.

Voices of Civil Rights
http://www.voicesofcivilrights.org/index.html
AARP, the Leadership Conference on Civil Rights (LCCR), and the Library of Congress have teamed up to collect and preserve personal accounts of America's struggle to fulfill the promise of equality for all.

We Shall Overcome
http://www.cr.nps.gov/nr/travel/civilrights/
National Register of Historic Places Travel Itinerary tells the powerful story of how and where the centuries-long struggle of African Americans to achieve the bright promise of America culminated in the mid-20th century in a heroic campaign we call the modern civil rights movement.

Topic: Martin Luther King, Jr.

Middle School Library Pathfinder

Pathfinders are guides which are intended to help you get started doing research on a particular topic, both online and at your library. Although these resources are useful as a starting point for your research, they are not the only resources that are available to you.

Definition/Introduction

■ *What is the topic? What does it cover?*

This pathfinder focuses on the life of Martin Luther King, Jr. and his role in the American Civil Rights Movement in the 1950s and 1960s.

■ *Catalog Subject Headings or Keywords*

King, Martin Luther, Jr.,1929-1968
Civil rights
Civil Rights Movement
Civil rights workers
Race relations
African Americans

■ *Dewey Numbers*

303.48 Causes of social change
323 Civil and political rights
323.4 Specific civil rights
973.92 United States history, 1953-2001

Print Resources

■ *Reference titles [dictionaries, encyclopedias, atlases, specific subject references]*

Crompton, Samuel Willard. *100 Spiritual Leaders Who Shaped World History.* Bluewood Books, c2001.

Encyclopedia of African-American Civil Rights: From Emancipation to the Present. Greenwood Press, c1992.

Hamilton, Neil A. *American Social Leaders and Activists.* Facts On File, c2002.

Pendergast, Tom. *The Sixties in America. Biographies.* UXL, Thomson/Gale, c2005.

■ *General titles [nonfiction, any suitable fiction]*

Be sure to check the library online catalog to find additional suitable materials.

Darby, Jean. *Martin Luther King, Jr.* Lerner Publications, c1990.

Gogerly, Liz. *The Dream of Martin Luther King: August 28, 1963.* Raintree Steck-Vaughn Publishers, c2004.

Hatt, Christine. *Martin Luther King Jr.* World Almanac Library, c2004.

Isaacs, Sally Senzell. *America in the Time of Martin Luther King Jr.: 1948-1976.* Heinemann Library, c2000.

Schloredt, Valerie. *Martin Luther King Jr.: Civil Rights Pioneer*. Blackbirch Press, Thomson/Gale, c2003.

Tate, Eleanora E. *Thank You, Dr. Martin Luther King, Jr.!* Bantam Doubleday Dell Books for Young Readers, c1997, c1990.

■ Journals

Be sure to check any online periodical database at your school library for more.

"Letter From Birmingham Jail". *Scholastic Scope*, 1/10/2005, Vol. 53 Issue 10, p14, 2p, 1bw

"The Power to Persuade". *Literary Cavalcade*, Jan2005, Vol. 57 Issue 4, p28, 3p, 1c

Rinaldo, Denise. "He Had a Dream". *Junior Scholastic*, 1/5/2004, Vol. 106 Issue 10, p8, 4p, 5bw

Web Resources

The King Center
http://thekingcenter.com
Information about Dr. King, the holiday named in his honor and his lasting legacy.

The Martin Luther King, Jr. Papers Project at Stanford University
http://www.stanford.edu/group/King/
Includes information about the Martin Luther King, Jr. Papers Projects at Stanford University, the King Estate, the King Center, and a listing of other related Web sites.

Martin Luther King, Jr., & the Civil Rights Movement
http://seattletimes.nwsource.com/mlk/
This site is provided by The Seattle Times to honor the memory of Martin Luther King, Jr. The site includes "stories and photos culled from The Seattle Times over the past decade."

Timeline of Events in Martin Luther King, Jr.'s Life
http://www.lib.lsu.edu/hum/mlk/srs216.html
Prepared by Louisiana State University to commemorate the life of Martin Luther King, Jr.

The U.S. Constitution Online
http://www.usconstitution.net/dream.html
The complete text of Dr. King's 1963 speech "I Have a Dream."

Topic: Countries/Travel

Definition/Introduction

- ### *What is the topic? What does it cover?*

  Ready to take a trip to a new and exciting location? First you must learn about the country so you will know what to expect. In this unit, we will research a country with an eye toward visiting. We will look not only at the history and geography of the country, but also at the culture.

- ### *Catalog Subject Headings or Keywords*

  Travel
  > *See also the names of specific countries.*

- ### *Dewey Numbers*

  910   Geography and travel
  940 – 990   History of specific countries

Print Resources

- ### *Reference titles [dictionaries, encyclopedias, atlases, specific subject references]*

  Countries and Their Cultures. Macmillan Reference USA, c2001.

  CultureGrams, 2005. ProQuest Information and Learning Co., c2004.

  Encyclopedic World Atlas: A-Z Country-By-Country Coverage. Oxford University Press, c2002.

  Junior Worldmark Encyclopedia of the Nations. UXL, Thomson/Gale, c2004.

  The Oxford Essential Geographical Dictionary. Berkley Books, c1999.

  Worldmark Encyclopedia of the Nations. Gale, Thomson/Gale, c2004.

- ### *General titles [nonfiction, any suitable fiction]*

  Be sure to check the library online catalog to find additional suitable materials.

  Ashman, Linda. *The Essential Worldwide Monster Guide.* Simon & Schuster Books for Young Readers, c2003.

  Bowden, Rob. *Tourism: Our Impact on the Planet.* Raintree, c2004.

  Bowers, Vivien. *Wow Canada!: Exploring This Land From Coast to Coast to Coast.* Maple Tree Press, Distributed in the U.S. by Firefly Books, c1999.

  Discovering World Cultures: The Middle East. Greenwood Press, c2004.

  Fischel, Emma. *Northern Europe.* Mason Crest Publishers, c2003.

  Gunderson, Cory Gideon. *Countries of the Middle East.* Abdo, c2004.

Social Studies

■ *Journals*

Be sure to check any online periodical database at your school library for more.

"5 More Undiscovered Treasures" *National Geographic Adventure,* Nov2004, Vol. 6 Issue 9, p28, 1/6p

Benoist, Michael. "Off the Inca Trail". *National Geographic Adventure*, Jun/Jul2004, Vol. 6 Issue 5, p20, 1p, 1 chart, 1 map, 1c

Kirby, Mark. "Insider Picks". *National Geographic Adventure*, Nov2004, Vol. 6 Issue 9, p26, 1/4p, 2c

Silver, Marc. "Flocking to Paradise". *U.S. News & World Report*, 11/22/2004, Vol. 137 Issue 18, pD4, 2p, 1 map, 3c

Smith, Alexander McCall. "My Number One Place in Africa". *National Geographic Traveler*, Sep2004, Vol. 21 Issue 6, p52, 2p, 2c

Web Resources

CIA World Factbook
http://www.cia.gov/cia/publications/factbook/
Includes maps, flags, and information on geography, people, government, communication, transportation, etc.

Country Studies From the Library of Congress
http://lcweb2.loc.gov/frd/cs/cshome.html
Online full-text versions provided by the Library of Congress.

Fodor's Travel Guides
http://www.fodors.com/
Fodor's travel guide online.

Geographic.Org
http://www.geographic.org
Includes information about people, maps, flags, and countries in easy-to-read fact sheets.

Geography IQ
http://www.geographyiq.com/
Find information on climate, weather, the economy, government, political, historical, and cultural traditions.

Lonely Planet Destinations
http://www.lonelyplanet.com/destinations/
Good place for the would-be traveler. Includes facts, attractions, environment, and when to go.

Topic: Immigration

Middle School Library Pathfinder

Pathfinders are guides which are intended to help you get started doing research on a particular topic, both online and at your library. Although these resources are useful as a starting point for your research, they are not the only resources that are available to you.

Definition/Introduction

■ *What is the topic? What does it cover?*

Since the first settlers landed in Virginia, America has been a destination for many immigrants. From all over the world, they traveled to the U.S. Their dreams may have varied – some came seeking fortune, some came seeking adventure, some came seeking freedom. The one thing that tied them all together is that America represented a dream for them.

■ *Catalog Subject Headings or Keywords*

Immigration and emigration
Immigrants
See also the names of the countries and nationalities of the immigrant group, e.g. Irish Americans.

■ *Dewey Numbers*

325.73 Immigrants to the United States

Print Resources

■ *Reference titles [dictionaries, encyclopedias, atlases, specific subject references]*

Daniels, Roger. *American Immigration: A Student Companion.* Oxford University Press, c2001.

Moreno, Barry. *Encyclopedia of Ellis Island.* Greenwood Press, c2004.

The Newest Americans. Greenwood Press, c2003.

Profiles In American History. UXL, c1994.

U.S. Immigration and Migration. UXL, Thomson/Gale, c2004.

■ *General titles [nonfiction, any suitable fiction]*

Be sure to check the library online catalog to find additional suitable materials.

Anderson, Dale. *Arriving at Ellis Island.* World Almanac Library, c2002.

Collier, Christopher. *A Century of Immigration: 1820-1924.* Benchmark Books, c2000.

Hoobler, Dorothy. *We Are Americans: Voices of the Immigrant Experience.* Scholastic Nonfiction, c2003.

Meltzer, Milton. *Bound for America: The Story of the European Immigrants.* Benchmark Books/Marshall Cavendish, c2002.

Rebman, Renee C. *Life on Ellis Island.* Lucent Books, c2000, c1999

■ *Journals*

Be sure to check any online periodical database at your school library for more.

"Coming To America". *Kids Discover*, May2002, Vol. 12 Issue 5, p2, 2p, 1c, 3bw

Gourley, Catherine. "The Passage Through Ellis Island: Immigrants' Own Stories". *Writing*, Apr/May2000, Vol. 22 Issue 6, p10, 3p, 3c, 1bw

Kowalski, Kathiann M. "A Better Life". *Cobblestone*, May2003, Vol. 24 Issue 5, p15, 5p, 1c, 4bw

"Waves of Immigration". *Scholastic News—Senior Edition*, 12/13/99 Map Skills Practice, Vol. 68 Issue 12, p10, 2p, 1bw

Web Resources

The American Immigrations Home Page
http://www.bergen.org/AAST/Projects/Immigration/
The American Immigrations Home Page was started as a part of a school project for a 10th grade American History Class. The project was meant to give information as to how immigrants not only were treated, but also why they decided to come to America.

Angel Island Immigration Station History
http://www.aiisf.org/history
Angel Island is sometimes called the Ellis Island of the west. It played a major role in the settlement of the West, serving both as a Public Health Service Quarantine Station, and an Immigration Station.

The Chinese in California 1850-1925
http://memory.loc.gov/ammem/award99/cubhtml/cichome.html
"The Chinese in California, 1850-1925 illustrates nineteenth and early twentieth century Chinese immigration to California through about 8,000 images and pages of primary source materials."

Interactive Tour of Ellis Island
http://teacher.scholastic.com/activities/immigration/tour/index.htm
See the layout of the processing center and journey with the immigrants as they enter the United States.

Lock and Walnut Grove: Havens for Early Asian Immigrants in California
http://www.cr.nps.gov/nr/twhp/wwwlps/lessons/locke/locke.htm
Here, in the Sacramento County delta area, where the San Joaquin and Sacramento Rivers converge, the history of the once bustling Chinatowns and *nihonmachi's* (Japan towns) can still be seen in buildings constructed some 50 to 100 years ago.

The New Americans
http://www.pbs.org/independentlens/newamericans/
Follow a diverse group of immigrants and refugees as they leave their homes and families behind and learn what it means to be new Americans in the 21st century.

Topic: Native Americans

Definition/Introduction

■ *What is the topic? What does it cover?*

Native Americans are descendants of the first people to live in the Americas. They had been living there for thousands of years before any Europeans arrived.

■ *Catalog Subject Headings or Keywords*

Indians of North America
Native peoples
First peoples
See also names of individuals and tribes.

■ *Dewey Numbers*

970.04 Indians of North America

Print Resources

■ *Reference titles [dictionaries, encyclopedias, atlases, specific subject references]*

America Indian Portraits. Macmillan Reference USA, c2000.

American Indian Tribes. Salem Press, c2000.

The Gale Encyclopedia of Native American Tribes. Gale, c1998.

Hakim, Joy. *The First Americans*. Oxford University Press, c2003.

Johnson, Michael. *Macmillan Encyclopedia of Native American Tribes*. Macmillan Library Reference USA, c1999.

Student Almanac Of Native American History. Greenwood Press, c2003.

■ *General titles [nonfiction, any suitable fiction]*

Be sure to check the library online catalog to find additional suitable materials.

Allen, Paula Gunn. *As Long As the Rivers Flow: The Stories of Nine Native Americans*. Scholastic, c2001, c1996.

Brown, Gene. *Discovery and Settlement: Europe Meets the New World, 1490-1700*. Twenty-First Century Books, c1993.

Collier, Christopher. *Clash of Cultures: Prehistory-1638*. Benchmark Books, c1998.

McCormick, Anita Louise. *Native Americans and the Reservation in American History*. Enslow Publishers, c1996.

Monceaux, Morgan. *My Heroes, My People: African Americans and Native Americans in the West*. Frances Foster Books, c1999.

Murdoch, David Hamilton. *North American Indian*. DK Publishers, c2000.

Nardo, Don. *The Native Americans*. Lucent Books, Thomson/Gale, c2003.

Steins, Richard. *Exploration and Settlement*. Raintree Steck-Vaughn, c2000.

▪ *Journals*

Be sure to check any online periodical database at your school library for more.

Bethune, Brian. "Mystery of the First North Americans". (cover story) *Maclean's*, 03/19/2001, Vol. 114 Issue 12, p24, 6p, 1 map, 10c

"Indian Removal and the Trail of Tears". *American History & Politics, 1607-1849*, 2002, p54, 2p

Smith, Steph. "Living Tribute". (cover story) *Scholastic News—Senior Edition*, 11/1/2004, Vol. 73 Issue 7, p4, 2p, 2c

Tayac, Gabrielle. "We Rise, We Fall, We Rise" (cover story) *Smithsonian*, Sep2004, Vol. 35 Issue 6, p63, 2p, 3c

Web Resources

American Indian History as told by American Indians
http://www.manataka.org/page10.html
The telling of stories is the essence of Indian culture. What better way to hear the stories than from the Indians themselves.

First Americans
http://jamaica.u.arizona.edu/ic/kmartin/School/index.htm
Links to information about the tribes and history of Native Americans.

Judgment Day
http://www.pbs.org/wgbh/aia/part4/4p2959.html
With settlers moving further and further west, the need for land increased. This led to the government taking the land from the Native Americans and forcing them to leave.

Native American Indian Resources
http://www.kstrom.net/isk/mainmenu.html
Links to all sorts of information about Native Americans.

WWW Virtual Library – American Indians
http://www.hanksville.org/NAresources/
Index of Native American resources on the Internet.

Topic: Women's History

Middle School Library Pathfinder

Pathfinders are guides which are intended to help you get started doing research on a particular topic, both online and at your library. Although these resources are useful as a starting point for your research, they are not the only resources that are available to you.

Definition/Introduction

- ### *What is the topic? What does it cover?*

  Much of written history focuses on the contributions of men. The study of women's roles in our history has been written about sparingly. This unit will focus on the contributions of women throughout history.

- ### *Catalog Subject Headings or Keywords*

  Women – History
  Feminism
  Women's history

- ### *Dewey Numbers*

  305.409 Historical, geographic, persons treatment
  305.4 Interdisciplinary works on women

Print Resources

- ### *Reference titles [dictionaries, encyclopedias, atlases, specific subject references]*

  Harness, Cheryl. *Remember the Ladies: 100 Great American Women.* HarperCollins, c2001.

  Heinemann, Sue. *The New York Public Library Amazing Women in American History: A Book of Answers for Kids.* John Wiley, c1998.

  Keenan, Sheila. *Scholastic Encyclopedia of Women in the United States.* Scholastic Reference, c2002.

  Leon, Vicki. *Uppity Women of the New World.* Conari Press, c2001.

  Women in World History: A Biographical Encyclopedia. Yorkin Publications , Gale Group, c2002, c1999.

- ### *General titles [nonfiction, any suitable fiction]*

  Be sure to check the library online catalog to find additional suitable materials.

  Bausum, Ann. *With Courage and Cloth: Winning the Fight for a Woman's Right to Vote.* National Geographic Society, c2004.

  Caravantes, Peggy. *Petticoat Spies: Six Women Spies of the Civil War.* Morgan Reynolds Publishers, c2002.

  Colman, Penny. *Rosie the Riveter: Women Working on the Home Front in World War II.* Crown, c1995.

  Hazell, Rebecca. *Heroines: Great Women Through the Ages.* Abbeville Press, c1996.

  Kendall, Martha E. *Failure Is Impossible!: The History of American Women's Rights.* Lerner Publications, c2001.

Leon, Vicki. *Outrageous Women of Ancient Times*. John Wiley, c1998.

Leon, Vicki. *Outrageous Women of the Middle Ages*. John Wiley, c1998.

Miller, Brandon Marie. *Good Women of a Well-Blessed Land: Women's Lives in Colonial America*. Lerner Publications, c2003.

■ *Journals*

Be sure to check any online periodical database at your school library for more.

Feddoes, Sadie. "Recognizing women's strengths and contributions". *New York Amsterdam News,* 3/21/2002, Vol. 93 Issue 12, p9, 2/5p, 1bw

Juhlin, Emma. "The World of Women". *Skipping Stones,* Jan/Feb2004, Vol. 16 Issue 1, p11, 2p

Upadhyay, Ritu. "A Place of Their Own". *Time for Kids,* 09/29/2000, Vol. 6 Issue 4, p7, 1/2p, 2c

Web Resources

Distinguished Women of Past and Present
http://www.distinguishedwomen.com/
This site has biographies of women who contributed to our culture in many different ways.

National Women's Hall of Fame
http://www.greatwomen.org/
Information about some of the greatest women in the history of this country.

Time for Kids Women's History Month
http://www.timeforkids.com/TFK/specials/articles/0,6709,101044,00.html
Information about Women's History Month and the women who are celebrated.

Women in American History
http://search.eb.com/women/
Information from Encyclopaedia Britannica.

Women in History
http://www.lkwdpl.org/wihohio/figures.htm
Living vignettes of women from the past.

Topic: African American History

Definition/Introduction

Pathfinders are guides which are intended to help you get started doing research on a particular topic, both online and at your library. Although these resources are useful as a starting point for your research, they are not the only resources that are available to you.

- *What is the topic? What does it cover?*

  The first African Americans in the United States did not come voluntarily. They came as slaves and struggled long and hard for their freedom. They have gone on to become a vital part of our society.

- *Catalog Subject Headings or Keywords*

  African Americans
  Afro-Americans
  Blacks
  See also names of individuals and various occupations.

- *Dewey Numbers*

  305.896 Africans and people of African descent
  973 General United States history

Print Resources

- *Reference titles [dictionaries, encyclopedias, atlases, specific subject references]*

  African American Almanac. UXL, c1994.

  African American Chronology. UXL, c1994.

  African-American Culture and History: A Student's Guide. Macmillan Reference USA, c2001.

  Encyclopedia of African-American Culture and History. Macmillan Library Reference USA, Simon & Schuster Macmillan, c1996.

  Hornsby, Alton. *Chronology of African American History: From 1492 to the Present.* Gale Research, c1997.

- *General titles [nonfiction, any suitable fiction]*

  Be sure to check the library online catalog to find additional suitable materials.

  Frankel, Noralee. *Break Those Chains At Last: African Americans, 1860-1880.* Oxford University Press, c1996.

  Grant, R.G. *The African-American Slave Trade.* Barron's, c2003.

  Lester, Julius. *From Slave Ship to Freedom Road.* Dial Books, c1998.

  Patrick-Wexler, Diane. *The New York Public Library Amazing African American History: A Book of Answers for Kids.* John Wiley, c1998.

Rhym, Darren. *The NAACP*. Chelsea House, c2002.

Somerlott, Robert. *The Little Rock School Desegregation Crisis in American History*. Enslow Publishers, c2001.

Taylor, Susie King. *The Diary of Susie King Taylor, Civil War Nurse*. Benchmark Books/Marshall Cavendish, c2004.

■ Journals

Be sure to check any online periodical database at your school library for more.

"The Fight to Have a Voice". *Scholastic News—Senior Edition*, 2/7/2005, Vol. 73 Issue 14, p6, 1p, 1c

"They paved the way". *USA Today*, 01/05/2005

Tibbitts, Tim. "A History Ingenuity". *Footsteps*, Jan/Feb2005, Vol. 7 Issue 1, p2, 5p, 1 diagram, 3c

Web Resources

African Americans in History
http://www.uga.edu/~iaas/History.html
Brief biographical sketches of several key figures in African American history.

Afro-American History
http://www.aawc.com/Zaah.html
The record of a race of indomitable people surviving the Diaspora.

The Faces of Science: African Americans in the Sciences
http://www.princeton.edu/~mcbrown/display/faces.html
Profiled here are African American men and women who have contributed to the advancement of science and engineering.

Historical Text Archive
http://historicaltextarchive.com/sections.php?op=listarticles&secid=8
A list of Internet links on the African-American experience divided by State and Region; People; Military; Slavery; and Arts & Entertainment.

Internet African American History Challenge
http://www.brightmoments.com/blackhistory/
"The Internet African American History Challenge[©] is an interactive quiz that helps you sharpen your knowledge of African American History."

Topic: Hispanic American Culture

Definition/Introduction

■ *What is the topic? What does it cover?*

The study of Hispanic American culture is difficult because a single, common Hispanic culture does not exist. There are, however, important similarities among Hispanic groups, who together strongly influence U.S. culture.

■ *Catalog Subject Headings or Keywords*

Hispanic Americans
Latin Americans
Mexican Americans
Spanish Americans

■ *Dewey Numbers*

305.868 Spanish Americans
973 General history of United States

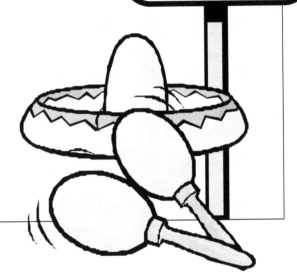

Middle School Library Pathfinder

Pathfinders are guides which are intended to help you get started doing research on a particular topic, both online and at your library. Although these resources are useful as a starting point for your research, they are not the only resources that are available to you.

Print Resources

■ *Reference titles [dictionaries, encyclopedias, atlases, specific subject references]*

Coerver, Don M. *Mexico: An Encyclopedia of Contemporary Culture and History.* ABC-CLIO, c2004.

Kanellos, Nicolas. *Hispanic Firsts: 500 Years of Extraordinary Achievement.* Visible Ink Press, c1997.

Gale Encyclopedia of Multicultural America. Gale Group, c2000.

UXL Hispanic American Almanac. UXL, Thomson/Gale, c2003.

Worldmark Encyclopedia of Cultures and Daily Life. Gale Group, c1998.

■ *General titles [nonfiction, any suitable fiction]*

Be sure to check the library online catalog to find additional suitable materials.

Hill, Christine M. *Ten Hispanic American Authors.* Enslow Publishers, c2002.

Laezman, Rick. *100 Hispanic Americans Who Changed History.* World Almanac Library, c2005.

Nickles, Greg. *The Hispanics.* Crabtree, c2001.

Ochoa, George. *The New York Public Library Amazing Hispanic American History: A Book of Answers For Kids.* John Wiley, c1998.

Sanchez, Richard. *The Fight For Civil Rights and a New Freedom.* Abdo, c1994.

St. John, Jetty. *Hispanic Scientists.* Capstone Press, c1996.

Student Almanac of Hispanic American History. Greenwood Press, c2004.

■ *Journals*

Be sure to check any online periodical database at your school library for more.

Haubegger, Christy. "The Legacy of Generation N". (cover story) *Newsweek*, 07/12/99, Vol. 134 Issue 2, p61, 1p, 2c

Larmer, Brook; Chambers, Veronica; Figueroa, Ana; Wingert, Pat; Weingarten, Julie. "Latino America". (cover story) *Newsweek*, 07/12/99, Vol. 134 Issue 2, p48, 4p, 15 graphs, 1 map, 2c

Leland, John; Chambers, Veronica; Figueroa, Ana; Clemetson, Lynette; Wingert, Pat; Weingarden, Julie; Hayden, Thomas; Brant, Martha. "Generation N". (cover story) *Newsweek*, 07/12/99, Vol. 134 Issue 2, p52, 7p, 13c

Web Resources

Hispanic America U.S.A.
http://www.neta.com/~1stbooks/
Web site includes pictures, documents, and links about Hispanic Americans.

Thomson Gale Hispanic Heritage
http://www.gale.com/free_resources/chh/index.htm
Hispanic Heritage Month free resource site. Thomson Gale has assembled a collection of activities and information to complement classroom topics.

U.S, Latino History and Culture
http://www.si.edu/resource/faq/nmah/latino.htm
Resources and selected links to Latino art and culture.

Topic: U.S. Presidents

Definition/Introduction

- ### *What is the topic? What does it cover?*

  After America won its independence from Great Britain, a new form of government was created. The Americans did not want a king as they had while part of Great Britain, but wanted to be able to choose a leader, but not for life. The people would elect a new president every few years and eliminate the possibility of being stuck with a ruler who was not popular or not doing his job. The president of the United States is considered the most powerful elected official in the world.

- ### *Catalog Subject Headings or Keywords*

  Presidents – United States
  > *See also the names of individual presidents.*

- ### *Dewey Numbers*

  973 United States history

Print Resources

- ### *Reference titles [dictionaries, encyclopedias, atlases, specific subject references]*

  Kane, Joseph Nathan. *Facts About the Presidents.* H.W. Wilson, c2001.
  American Presidents in World History. Greenwood Press, c2003.
  The Complete History of Our Presidents. Rourke Corp., c2001, c1997.

- ### *General titles [nonfiction, any suitable fiction]*

  Be sure to check the library online catalog to find additional suitable materials.
  See the names of individual presidents.
  See also general history books about the time period.

- ### *Journals*

  Be sure to check any online periodical database at your school library for more.
  Search for the names of individual presidents.

Web Resources

American Presidency: A Glorious Burden
http://americanhistory.si.edu/presidency/home.html
Information about the campaign trails, the life and death in the White House. Click on timeline to view the order of presidency.

American Presidents: Life Portraits
http://www.americanpresidents.org/
The American Presidents Web site, created for the television series, contains a complete video archive of all American Presidents: Life Portraits programming.

Genealogy of the U.S. Presidents
http://www3.dcs.hull.ac.uk/genealogy/presidents/presidents.html
This database is a Web-browsable version of the published Gedcom of the genealogy of the U.S. presidents.

Grolier's Online: The American Presidency
http://gi.grolier.com/presidents/
Links to history of presidents, the presidency, politics, and related subjects. Includes multimedia clips, biographies with inaugural addresses, elections, and much more!

Internet Public Library: POTUS:
http://www.ipl.org/div/potus/
Information on each president. Also has links to biographies, historical documents, and other presidential sites.

PBS The Presidents
http://www.pbs.org/wgbh/amex/presidents/index.html
"The Presidents Web site builds on the enormous collection of research materials developed for the award-winning broadcasts. The site includes a summary page for each chief executive, provides featured Presidents, an in-depth look at the presidents in the broadcast series line-up, and includes resources such as links to presidential sites, a detailed bibliography and a comprehensive collection of primary sources."

President Information From Information Please
http://infoplease.kids.lycos.com/ipka/A0777337.html
Includes burial places, occupations, and information on wives and children.

White House Web Site – First Ladies' Gallery
http://www.whitehouse.gov/history/firstladies/
Information about the first ladies in order by date.

White House Web Site – Presidents of the United States
http://www.whitehouse.gov/history/presidents/gw1.html
Includes famous quotes from each president.

Topic: World Religions

Middle School Library Pathfinder

Pathfinders are guides which are intended to help you get started doing research on a particular topic, both online and at your library. Although these resources are useful as a starting point for your research, they are not the only resources that are available to you.

Definition/Introduction

■ *What is the topic? What does it cover?*

Religion often defines humans' code of beliefs. This code of belief has sometimes caused us to become closer with others. It has also led to major conflicts.

■ *Catalog Subject Headings or Keywords*

Religion
> *See also specific religions, e.g. Hinduism, Christianity.*

■ *Dewey Numbers*

200 Browse the whole section

Print Resources

■ *Reference titles [dictionaries, encyclopedias, atlases, specific subject references]*

Comparative Religions on File. Facts On File, c2000.

The Encyclopedia of World Religions. Facts On File, c1998.

Myths and Legends of the World. Macmillan Reference USA, c2000.

The Wilson Chronology of the World's Religions. H.W. Wilson Co., c2000.

Web Resources

Religions of the World
http://emuseum.mnsu.edu/cultural/religion/
World eligions and their beliefs.

Your Guide to the Religions of the World
http://www.bbc.co.uk/worldservice/people/features/world_religions/index.shtml
World religions and their beliefs from the BBC. Alphabetical list of religions.

(Buddhist)
Buddhism: An Introduction
http://www.pbs.org/edens/thailand/buddhism.htm
Learn more about the Buddha, the four noble truths, karma, and the cycle of rebirth at this site from PBS.

(Catholic)
Catholic Encyclopedia
http://www.newadvent.org/cathen/
A wealth of information about Catholic doctrine and history.

(Christianity)
What is Christianity?
http://geneva.rutgers.edu/src/christianity/index.html
"This set of pages tries to summarize Christian beliefs and practices. It is intended as an introduction to Christianity for non-Christians."

(Confucianism)
Confucianism
http://www.religioustolerance.org/confuciu.htm
Site provides the basic beliefs of this religion.

(Druids)
Druids
http://religiousmovements.lib.virginia.edu/nrms/drud.html
Site provides a history of the religion, a brief summary of its beliefs, its organizational structure, and presents a summary of various issues and controversies in the faith's history.

(Hindu)
The Hindu Universe
http://www.hindunet.org/home.shtml
Hindu arts, customs, worship, history, and more.

(Islam)
Islam: Empire of Faith
http://www.pbs.org/empires/islam/
Information about Islamic faith and culture as well as profiles of famous leaders.

(Judaism)
Internet Jewish History Sourcebook
http://www.fordham.edu/halsall/jewish/jewishsbook.html
Site provides a comprehensive look at the history of Judaism throughout time.

(Sikhs)
Sikhs
http://religiousmovements.lib.virginia.edu/nrms/sikhs.html
Site provides a history of the religion, a brief summary of its beliefs, its organizational structure, and presents a summary of various issues and controversies in the faith's history.

(Taoism)
Taoism
http://religiousmovements.lib.virginia.edu/nrms/taoism.html
Site provides a history of the religion, a brief summary of its beliefs, its organizational structure, and presents a summary of various issues and controversies in the faith's history.

(Wicca)
Wicca
http://religiousmovements.lib.virginia.edu/nrms/wicca.html
Site provides a history of the religion, a brief summary of its beliefs, its organizational structure, and presents a summary of various issues and controversies in the faith's history.

Topic: Alternative Energy

Middle School Library Pathfinder

Pathfinders are guides which are intended to help you get started doing research on a particular topic, both online and at your library. Although these resources are useful as a starting point for your research, they are not the only resources that are available to you.

Definition/Introduction

- *What is the topic? What does it cover?*

  Alternative energy is energy derived from sources that are renewable or ecologically safe. These include water power, solar power, wind power, and geothermal power, among others.

- *Catalog Subject Headings or Keywords*

  Biomass fuel
  Car Pool
  Geothermal energy cars
  Hydro electric cars
  Nuclear energy
  Public transportation
  Renewable energy
  Solar energy
  Sustainable energy
  Wind

- *Dewey Numbers*

  333.79 Natural resources
  621.042 Applied physics

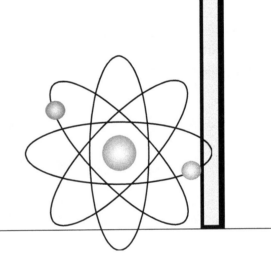

Print Resources

- *Reference titles [dictionaries, encyclopedias, atlases, specific subject references]*

  Bruno, Leonard C. *Science and Technology Breakthroughs: From the Wheel to the World Wide Web.* UXL, c1998.

  Macmillan Encyclopedia of the Environment. Macmillan Library Reference USA, c1997.

- *General titles [nonfiction, any suitable fiction]*

  Be sure to check the library online catalog to find additional suitable materials.

  Bowden, Rob. *Energy.* Kidhaven Press, Thomson/Gale, c2004.

  Morgan, Sally. *Alternative Energy Sources.* Heinemann Library, c2003.

  Stille, Darlene R. *Natural Resources—Using and Protecting Earth's Supplies.* Compass Point Books, c2005.

  Watson, Susan. *Living Sustainably.* Smart Apple Media, c2004, c2003.

■ *Journals*

Be sure to check any online periodical database at your school library for more.

Carey, John. "Alternative Energy Gets Real". *Business Week,* 12/27/2004 Issue 3,914, p106, 2p, 1 chart, 1c

Coleman-Lochner, Lauren. "Huge effort needed for alternative fuels to work". *USA Today,* 11/17/2003

Foroohar, Rana. "Eclipse of the Sun". *Newsweek*, 9/20/2004, Vol. 144 Issue 12, pE37, 1/2p, 1c

Kharif, Olga; Steve Rosenbush. "Racing to Energy's Great Green Future." *Business Week Online*, 10/8/2004, pN.PAG, 00p

Web Resources

Alternative Fuels Data Center
http://www.eere.energy.gov/afdc/
The Alternative Fuels Data Center is a vast collection of information on alternative fuels and the vehicles that use them.

Energy Information Administration
http://www.eia.doe.gov/
Official Energy Statistics from the U.S. Government.

I Got the Power: Alternative Energy Resources on the Web
http://www.infotoday.com/searcher/may01/mcdermott.htm
Site has information and links to alternative energy resources.

Renewable Resource Data Center (RReDC)
http://rredc.nrel.gov/
The RReDC is supported by the National Center for Photovoltaics (NCPV) and managed by the Department of Energy's Office of Energy Efficiency and Renewable Energy.

Topic: Chemical Elements

Definition/Introduction

■ *What is the topic? What does it cover?*

Any substance that cannot be decomposed into simpler substances by ordinary chemical processes is a chemical element.

■ *Catalog Subject Headings or Keywords*

Chemical elements
Periodic law
Elements
Element, chemical
    See also names of specific elements, e.g. Hydrogen.

■ *Dewey Numbers*

546 Inorganic chemistry
541 Physical chemistry

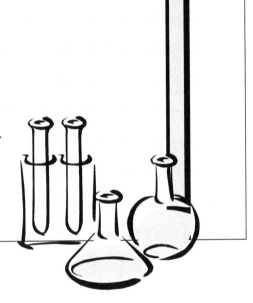

Print Resources

■ *Reference titles [dictionaries, encyclopedias, atlases, specific subject references]*

Newton, David E. *Chemical Elements: From Carbon to Krypton.* UXL, c1999.

Stwertka, Albert. *A Guide to the Elements.* Oxford University Press, c2002.

■ *General titles [nonfiction, any suitable fiction]*

Be sure to check the library online catalog to find additional suitable materials.

Baldwin, Carol. *Mixtures, Compounds & Solutions.* Raintree, c2004.

Krasnow, David. *Elements.* G. Stevens Pub., c2003.

Oxlade, Chris. *Elements & Compounds.* Heinemann Library, c2002.

Parker, Steve. *Chemicals & Change.* Chelsea House, c2005.

White, Katherine. *Mendeleyev and the Periodic Table.* Rosen Central Primary Source, c2005.

■ *Journals*

Be sure to check any online periodical database at your school library for more.

Adams, Jacqueline. "Name That Element". *Science World*, 1/24/2005, Vol. 61 Issue 8, p20, 3p, 2c

"New Elements Made". *Current Science*, 4/16/2004, Vol. 89 Issue 15, p13, 1/2p, 1c

"Periodic Table of Elements". *World Almanac & Book of Facts*, 2004, p684, 1p, 1 graphic

Svoboda, Elizabeth. "Two New Elements Discovered". *Discover*, Jan2005, Vol. 26 Issue 1, p38, 1/3p

Web Resources

Chemical Elements and Symbols Quiz
http://quizhub.com/quiz/f-elements.cfm
Interactive quiz on the elements. Give it a try and see how much you really know.

Chemical Elements.com
http://www.chemicalelements.com
Interactive periodic table. Created as an eighth grade project!

WebElements Periodic Table
http://www.webelements.com
Interactive periodic table.

Topic: Light and Optics

Definition/Introduction

- *What is the topic? What does it cover?*

  Optics is the branch of physics that deals with the study of light and vision.

- *Catalog Subject Headings or Keywords*

  Light
  Optics

- *Dewey Numbers*

  535 Visible light

Print Resources

- *Reference titles [dictionaries, encyclopedias, atlases, specific subject references]*

  Kerrod, Robin. *The Way Science Works*. DK Publishing, c2002.
  The Young Oxford Library of Science. Oxford University Press, c2002, c2001.

- *General titles [nonfiction, any suitable fiction]*

  Be sure to check the library online catalog to find additional suitable materials.
  Fullick, Ann. *Seeing Things: Light*. Heinemann Library, c2005.
  Gardner, Robert. *Optics*. Twenty-First Century Books, c1994.
  Levine, Shar. *The Optics Book: Fun Experiments with Light, Vision & Color*. Sterling, c1998.
  Parker, Steve. *Light and Sound*. Raintree Steck-Vaughn, c2001, c2000.

- *Journals*

  Be sure to check any online periodical database at your school library for more.
  "Jiggle Optics". *Scholastic SuperScience*, Nov/Dec2001, Vol. 13 Issue 3, p14, 1p, 1c
  "Seeing the Light". *Kids Discover*, May2004, Vol. 14 Issue 5, p2, 2p

Web Resources

How Light Works by Craig Freudenrich
http://www.howstuffworks.com/light.htm
Looks at light from many different angles to show you exactly how it works.

Light and Optics
http://ww2010.atmos.uiuc.edu/%28Gh%29/guides/mtr/opt/home.rxml
Investigates particle-light interactions and the assortment of optical effects they produce.

Light, Reflection and Refraction
http://acept.la.asu.edu/PiN/mod/light/reflection/pattLight1.html
The goal of this exercise is to come to terms with the concept of "light" and to explore some of the properties of this ever-present phenomenon.

Optics for Kids
http://www.opticalres.com/kidoptx.html
Some fun and interesting things about optics and the science of light.

Topic: Astronomy

Definition/Introduction

- ### *What is the topic? What does it cover?*

  Astronomy is the study of celestial bodies including the sun, the moon, the planets, stars, and galaxies.

- ### *Catalog Subject Headings or Keywords*

  Astronomy
  Physical sciences
  Space
  Stars
  Sky
  Outer space
  Planets

- ### *Dewey Numbers*

  520   Astronomy

Print Resources

- ### *Reference titles [dictionaries, encyclopedias, atlases, specific subject references]*

  Angelo, Joseph A. *The Fact On File Space and Astronomy Handbook.* Facts On File, c2002.

  Engelbert, Phillis. *Astronomy & Space: From the Big Bang to the Big Crunch.* UXL, c1997.

  Lambert, David. *Earth Science on File.* Facts On File, c2004.

  Pascoe, Elaine. *Scholastic Kid's Almanac: Facts, Figures, and Stats.* Scholastic Reference, c2004.

  Space and Astronomy On File. Facts On File, c2001.

  Space Sciences. Macmillan Reference USA, Thomson/Gale, c2002.

  Todd, Deborah. *A to Z of Scientists in Space and Astronomy.* Facts On File, c2005.

- ### *General titles [nonfiction, any suitable fiction]*

  Be sure to check the library online catalog to find additional suitable materials.

  Cobb, Allan B. *How Do We Know How Stars Shine.* Rosen Pub. Group, c2001.

  Cole, Michael D. *Hubble Space Telescope: Exploring the Universe.* Enslow Publishers, c1999.

  Fredette, Nathalie. *Exploring the Universe.* World Almanac Library, c2001.

  Gallant, Roy A. *The Life Stories of Stars.* Benchmark Books, c2000.

  Reed, George. *Eyes on the Universe.* Benchmark Books, c2001.

Silverstein, Alvin. *The Universe.* Twenty-First Century Books, c2003.

Spangenburg, Ray. *Observing the Universe.* Franklin Watts, c2003.

■ *Journals*

Be sure to check any online periodical database at your school library for more.

Bakich, Michael E. "Stars and the Dusty Disks Around Them". *Astronomy*, Mar2005, Vol. 33 Issue 3, p26, 1/3p, 1c

Berman, Bob. "Is It Raining Asteroids?" *Discover*, Dec2004, Vol. 25 Issue 12, p28, 1p

Croswell, Ken. "'New' Star Found Near Sol". *Astronomy*, Mar2005, Vol. 33 Issue 3, p30, 1/2p, 1c

Villard, Ray. "The Weirdest Star in the Sky". *Astronomy*, Mar2005, Vol. 33 Issue 3, p34, 6p, 9c

Web Resources

NASA
http://www.nasa.gov/home/index.html
Absolutely loaded with great information about space.

The Nine Planets
http://www.nineplanets.org/
A multimedia tour of the solar system.

Virtual Solar System
http://www.nationalgeographic.com/solarsystem/
Discover the wonders of our solar system in a spectacular 3-D environment.

Welcome to the Planets
http://pds.jpl.nasa.gov/planets/
This is a collection of many of the best images from NASA's planetary exploration program.

Topic: Earthquakes

Definition/Introduction

- ### What is the topic? What does it cover?

  A shaking of the Earth's surface from a build up of stress of the plates beneath the surface results in an earthquake.

- ### Catalog Subject Headings or Keywords

  Earthquakes
  Seismology
  Natural disasters
  Physical geography

- ### Dewey Numbers

  551.22 Earthquakes

Print Resources

- ### Reference titles [dictionaries, encyclopedias, atlases, specific subject references]

  Davis, Lee. *Natural Disasters*. Facts On File, c2002.

  Engelbert, Phillis. *Dangerous Planet: The Science of Natural Disasters*. UXL, c2001.

  History's Most Devastating Disasters. Macmillan Reference USA, c2001.

  Ritchie, David. *Encyclopedia of Earthquakes and Volcanoes*. Facts On File, c2001.

- ### General titles [nonfiction, any suitable fiction]

  Be sure to check the library online catalog to find additional suitable materials.

  Colson, Mary. *Shaky Ground: Earthquakes*. Raintree, c2004.

  Gallant, Roy A. *Plates: Restless Earth*. Benchmark Books, c2003.

  Gallant, Roy A. *Structure: Exploring Earth's Interior*. Benchmark Books/Marshall Cavendish, c2003.

  Lassieur, Allison. *Earthquakes*. Capstone Books, c2001.

  Mehta-Jones, Shilpa. *Earthquake Alert!* Crabtree, c2004.

  Trueit, Trudi Strain. *Earthquakes*. Franklin Watts, c2003.

■ *Journals*

Be sure to check any online periodical database at your school library for more.

Skelton, Renee. "Earthquake!" *National Geographic for Kids*, Mar2004 Issue 338, p30, 2p, 1 map, 5c

Tompkins, Joshua. "Seismic Stakeout". *Popular Science*, Jul2004, Vol. 265 Issue 1, p32, 2p

Wilson, Jim. "Predicting Earthquakes From Space". Popular Mechanics, Dec2003, Vol. 180 Issue 12, p44, 2p, 1c

Web Resources

Earthquakes
http://www.thetech.org/exhibits_events/online/quakes/
Learn about earthquakes and the steps scientists are taking to predict them and how builders are building flexible structures that can withstand the strong shaking produced by earthquakes.

National Earthquake Information Center
http://wwwneic.cr.usgs.gov/
The mission of the National Earthquake Information Center (NEIC) is to rapidly determine location and size of all destructive earthquakes worldwide and to immediately disseminate this information to concerned national and international agencies, scientists, and the general public.

Understanding Earthquakes
http://www.crustal.ucsb.edu/ics/understanding/
So you think you know all about earthquakes. Then take the earthquake quiz or read some accounts of earthquakes from famous people.

United States Geological Survey Earthquake Web Site
http://earthquake.usgs.gov/
Information on worldwide earthquake activity, earthquake science, and earthquake hazard reduction.

Worldwide Earthquake Activity
http://neic.usgs.gov/neis/bulletin/bulletin.html
Get the latest information about where earthquakes are occurring.

Topic: El Niño

Definition/Introduction

- **What is the topic? What does it cover?**

  El Niño causes a warm ocean surge. This in turn causes the trade winds to cease so that the cool ocean currents driven by them stop. This process can disrupt the climate.

- **Catalog Subject Headings or Keywords**

  El Niño
  Weather
  Climate
  El Niño current

- **Dewey Numbers**

  551.6 Climatology and weather

Print Resources

- **Reference titles [dictionaries, encyclopedias, atlases, specific subject references]**

  The DK Science Encyclopedia. DK Publishing, c1998.

  Junior Science On File. Facts On File, c1991.

- **General titles [nonfiction, any suitable fiction]**

  Be sure to check the library online catalog to find additional suitable materials.

  Arnold, Caroline. *El Niño Stormy Weather for People and Wildlife*. Clarion, c2005.

  Scoones, Simon. *Climate Change: Our Impact on the Planet*. Raintree Steck-Vaughn, c2002.

- **Journals**

  Be sure to check any online periodical database at your school library for more.

  Patrick O'Driscoll. "El Niño Is Brewing Wet Winter For South". *USA Today*, 10/07/2004

  Perkins, S. "Weather Wise". *Science News*, 4/17/2004, Vol. 165 Issue 16, p243, 1/2p

  S. P. "Twin Satellites Track Water's Rise And Fall". *Science News*, 8/7/2004, Vol. 166 Issue 6, p94, 1/5p

  "What is El Niño?" *World Almanac for Kids*, 2005, p295, 1/2p, 1c

Web Resources

Center for Ocean-Atmospheric Perdition Studies
http://www.coaps.fsu.edu/lib/elninolinks/
Includes full text articles online and bibliographies.

Hot Air Over Hot Water
http://www.fi.edu/weather/nino/nino.html
Information about El Niño.

NOAA El Niño Page
http://www.elnino.noaa.gov/
NOAA is the National Oceanic and Atmospheric Administration, which has primary responsibilities for providing forecasts to the Nation, and a leadership role in sponsoring El Niño observations and research.

Nova El Niño Tracking
http://www.pbs.org/wgbh/nova/elnino/
Next to the seasons, El Niño is the most powerful force driving global weather. Find out what scientists are learning about this mysterious weather phenomenon and its reach through space and time.

USA Today Weather
http://www.usatoday.com/weather/resources/basics/wnino0.htm
Resources for El Niño and La Niña.

U.S. Department of Commerce/NOAA /PMEL/TAO/El Niño Theme Page
http://www.pmel.noaa.gov/tao/elnino/el-nino-story.html
Explanation with graphics from the Pacific Environmental Laboratory of the National Oceanic and Atmospheric Administration.

The Wrath of El Niño
http://www.pbs.org/newshour/forum/october97/el_nino_10-3.html
The National Weather Service held an Online Forum on PBS Newshour.

WW2010 – El Niño
http://ww2010.atmos.uiuc.edu/(Gh)/guides/mtr/eln/home.rxml
WW2010 (the weather world 2010 project). Comprehensive information about El Niño.

Topic: Hurricanes

Middle School Library Pathfinder

Pathfinders are guides which are intended to help you get started doing research on a particular topic, both online and at your library. Although these resources are useful as a starting point for your research, they are not the only resources that are available to you.

Definition/Introduction

- *What is the topic? What does it cover?*

  Hurricanes are violent, swirling storms that form over the warm ocean. When they hit land, they can be extremely destructive and cause damage and loss of life.

- *Catalog Subject Headings or Keywords*

  Natural disasters
  Hurricanes
  Hurricane protection
  See also names of specific hurricanes.

- *Dewey Numbers*

  551.55 Atmospheric disturbances and formations

Print Resources

- *Reference titles [dictionaries, encyclopedias, atlases, specific subject references]*

  Davis, Lee. *Natural Disasters*. Facts On File, c2002.

  Engelbert, Phillis. *Dangerous Planet: The Science of Natural Disasters*. UXL, c2001.

  The DK Science Encyclopedia. DK Publishing, c1998.

  History's Most Devastating Disasters. Macmillan Reference USA, c2001.

- *General titles [nonfiction, any suitable fiction]*

  Be sure to check the library online catalog to find additional suitable materials.

  Challoner, Jack. *Hurricane & Tornado*. DK Publishing, c2004.

  Galiano, Dean. *Hurricanes*. Rosen Central, c2000.

  Hirschmann, Kris. *Hurricanes*. Lucent Books, c2002.

  Oxlade, Chris. *Violent Skies: Hurricanes*. Raintree, c2005.

  Sakany, Lois. *Hurricane Hunters and Tornado Chasers: Life in the Eye of the Storm*. Rosen Central, 2003.

  Sherrow, Victoria. *Hurricane Andrew: Nature's Rage*. Enslow Publishers, c1998.

  Vaughan, Jenny. *Natural Disasters*. Franklin Watts, c1999.

■ *Journals*

Be sure to check any online periodical database at your school library for more.

"2004 Atlantic Hurricanes A Season of Devastation". *Weatherwise*, Mar/Apr2005, Vol. 58 Issue 2, p52, 10p

Halverson, Jeff. "A Hurricane is Born". *Weatherwise*, Nov/Dec2004, Vol. 57 Issue 6, p72, 2p, 1c

Smith, Tony. "Blown Away". *Scholastic Scope*, 12/13/2004, Vol. 53 Issue 9, p17, 3p, 2 charts, 1 map, 5c

Web Resources

American Red Cross Hurricane Safety Tips
http://www.redcross.org/services/disaster/0,1082,0_587_,00.html
Know what to expect in a hurricane, how to prepare, and what to do during and after a hurricane.

FEMA
http://www.fema.gov/hazards/hurricanes/
The Federal Emergency Management Agency's site about hurricanes.

Hurricane Watch Net
http://www.hwn.org/
Information about active storms and how to be prepared.

National Hurricane Center
http://www.nhc.noaa.gov/
Everything you need to know about hurricanes.

WFTV.com Hurricane site
http://html.wftv.com/sh/idi/weather/hurricanes/
Information about the anatomy, strength, location, history, and how hurricanes are named.

Topic: Landforms

Definition/Introduction

- ### *What is the topic? What does it cover?*

  Landforms are the creation and alteration of the natural features of the earth's surface.

- ### *Catalog Subject Headings or Keywords*

  Geology
  Landforms
  Earth
  Plate tectonics
  Mountains
  Volcanoes
  Earthquakes
  Erosion

- ### *Dewey Numbers*

  549 Mineralogy
  550 Earth sciences
  551 Geology, hydrology, meteorology

Print Resources

- ### *Reference titles [dictionaries, encyclopedias, atlases, specific subject references]*

  Nagel, Rob. *UXL Encyclopedia of Landforms and Other Geologic Features.* UXL, Thomson/Gale, c2004.

  Oldershaw, Cally. *Atlas of Geology and Landforms.* Franklin Watts, c2001.

- ### *General titles [nonfiction, any suitable fiction]*

  Be sure to check the library online catalog to find additional suitable materials.

  Land And Water. Gareth Stevens Pub., c2004.

  McClish, Bruce. *Island Continents & Supercontinents: Australia & Antarctica.* Heinemann Library, c2003.

  Our Planet Today. World Almanac Library, c2001.

■ *Journals*

Be sure to check any online periodical database at your school library for more.

"Land and Water". *Junior Scholastic*, 3/8/2004, Vol. 106 Issue 14, p20, 2p, 1 map

Perkins, Sid. "Patterns From Nowhere". *Science News*, 5/17/2003, Vol. 163 Issue 20, p314, 3p, 2c

Perkins, Sid. "Thin Skin". (cover story) *Science News*, 1/3/2004, Vol. 165 Issue 1, p11, 3p, 1c, 2bw

Web Resources

Continental Drift and Plate Tectonics
http://kids.earth.nasa.gov/archive/pangaea
Scientists believe that 200 million years ago the Earth's continents were joined together to form one gigantic supercontinent called Pangaea. As the rock plates that the continents sit on moved, the supercontinent broke up and began to move apart.

Illustrated Glossary: Landforms & Bodies of Water
http://www.enchantedlearning.com/geography/landforms/glossary.shtml
"This web site, from EnchantedLearning.com, features an illustrated glossary of a large number of landforms and bodies of water. Some terms are hyperlinked to other EnchantedLearning.com sites where students can find more information."

Investigation Earth Systems: Rock and Landforms
http://www.agiweb.org/ies/rock.html
Hands-on, inquiry based investigations to explore.

Landforms: Face of the Earth
http://www.edu.pe.ca/southernkings/landforms.htm
Includes information on the following landforms: valleys, plateaus, mountains, plains, hills, and glaciers.

U.S. Geological Survey – Student Resources
http://interactive2.usgs.gov/learningweb/students/index.htm
Contains project ideas, homework help, research tools, and more. Use the "basic search" feature on the right to quickly find specific information on your landform.

Topic: Minerals

Definition/Introduction

- *What is the topic? What does it cover?*

  Minerals are naturally formed inorganic substances with a particular chemical composition and an ordered internal structure.

- *Catalog Subject Headings or Keywords*

  Minerals
  Mines and mineral resources
  Petrology

- *Dewey Numbers*

  553 Economic geology
  549 Mineralogy

Print Resources

- *Reference titles [dictionaries, encyclopedias, atlases, specific subject references]*

  Macmillan Encyclopedia of the Environment. Macmillan Library Reference USA, c1997.

  Zim, Herbert Spencer. *Rocks, Gems, and Minerals: A Guide to Familiar Minerals, Gems, Ores and Rocks.* St. Martin's Press, c2001.

- *General titles [nonfiction, any suitable fiction]*

  Be sure to check the library online catalog to find additional suitable materials.

  Kittinger, Jo S. *A Look At Minerals: From Galena to Gold.* Franklin Watts, c1998.

  Prokos, Anna. *Rocks and Minerals.* Gareth Stevens Pub., c2004.

  Stille, Darlene R. *Minerals—From Apatite to Zinc (Exploring Science).* Compass Point Books, c2004.

  Symes, R. F. *Rocks & Minerals.* DK Publishing, c2004.

  Trueit, Trudi Strain. *Rocks, Gems, and Minerals.* Franklin Watts, c2003.

  Whyman, Kathryn. *Metals and the Environment.* Stargazer Books, c2005.

  The Illustrated Science Encyclopedia. Amazing Planet Earth. Southwater Press, Distributed in the USA by Anness Pub., c2001.

■ *Journals*

Be sure to check any online periodical database at your school library for more.

"Minerals, Rocks, and Gems". *World Almanac for Kids*, 2004, p194, 1/2p, 1c

Paffrath, April. "Collect Rocks". *Scientific American Explorations*, Summer2001, Vol. 4 Issue 3, p11, 1p, 1c

"What are minerals?" *Monkeyshines & Ewe Explore the 7 Continents*, 2001, p45, 1p, 1bw

Web Resources

The Mineral Gallery – Minerals by Name
http://mineral.galleries.com/minerals/by-name.htm
Explores rocks and minerals by name.

Mineralogy Database
http://webmineral.com/
Includes links to definitions of minerals as well as more than 4,000 mineral species descriptions.

Mineral Identification Site
http://www.netspace.net.au/~mwoolley/top.htm
"There are three main parts to this web site on mineral identification: About Minerals, How to Identify Minerals, and a Key to Identification. Each section contains more details that will help readers to understand what minerals are made of, where they can be found, and how they are used. A search engine on the site provides quick look-up key terms."

The Physical Characteristics of Minerals
http://mineral.galleries.com/minerals/physical.htm
"Did you know that minerals could be only identified absolutely by x-ray analysis and chemical tests? This web-site offers practical tests and information about identifying minerals. Viewers will find a list of minerals by class or by name, and there is also a link to interesting minerals such as gemstones and birthstones as well. View locations that made a name for themselves with mineral collectors!"

Topic: Oceans

Definition/Introduction

■ *What is the topic? What does it cover?*

Oceans cover approximately 70 percent of the Earth's surface and have fascinated man for many years. Much is known about the oceans and the animals that live there. But, much is yet a mystery to us as well.

■ *Catalog Subject Headings or Keywords*

Ocean
Oceanography

■ *Dewey Numbers*

551.46 Hydrosphere and submarine geology

Print Resources

■ *Reference titles [dictionaries, encyclopedias, atlases, specific subject references]*

Day, Trevor. *Exploring the Ocean.* Oxford University Press, c2003.

Nagel, Rob. *UXL Encyclopedia of Landforms and Other Geologic Features.* UXL, Thomson/Gale, c2004.

Junior Worldmark Encyclopedia of Physical Geography. UXL, Thomson/Gale, c2003.

Macmillan Encyclopedia of the Environment. Macmillan Library Reference USA, c1997.

Marine Science On File. Facts On File, c2001.

UXL Encyclopedia of Biomes. UXL, c2000.

■ *General titles [nonfiction, any suitable fiction]*

Be sure to check the library online catalog to find additional suitable materials.

Day, Trevor. *Oceans and Beaches.* Raintree Steck-Vaughn, c2003.

Lambert, David. *The Kingfisher Young People's Book of Oceans.* Kingfisher, c1997.

Marx, Christy. *Life in the Ocean Depths.* Rosen Central, c2004.

Oleksy, Walter G. *Mapping the Seas.* Franklin Watts, c2002.

Stefoff, Rebecca. *Ferdinand Magellan and the Discovery of the World Ocean.* Chelsea House, c1990.

Vogel, Carole Garbuny. *Human Impact.* Franklin Watts, c2003.

■ *Journals*

Be sure to check any online periodical database at your school library for more.

"One fish, two fish . . .". *Scholastic News—Senior Edition*, 11/10/2003, Vol. 72 Issue 8, p2, 2/3p, 2c

Perkins, S. "Sea Change". *Science News*, 7/17/2004, Vol. 166 Issue 3, p35, 2/3p, 1c

Safina, Carl; Chasis, Sarah. "Saving the Oceans". *Issues in Science & Technology*, Fall2004, Vol. 21 Issue 1, p37, 8p

Spotts, Peter N. "Tiniest Creatures May Reveal Health Of Oceans". *Christian Science Monitor*, 12/16/2004, Vol. 97 Issue 15, p13, 0p, 2c

Web Resources

Aquatic Network
http://www.aquanet.com/resources/ocean/aq_ocn3.htm
Links to information about the ocean biome.

Mystic Aquarium Institute for Exploration
http://www.mysticaquarium.org/animals/home/
"Come travel to the very deepest part of the ocean and share the fascinating discoveries of Dr. Robert Ballard and his team from the Institute for Exploration."

Oceans Fact Sheets
http://www.yoto98.noaa.gov/factshee.htm
Information about oceans including importance, animals, pollution, and more.

Sea and Sky
http://www.seasky.org/sea.html
Information about the oceans, exploration, and animals that you find there.

Secrets of the Ocean Realm
http://www.pbs.org/oceanrealm/seadwellers/
Now is your chance to get up close and personal with some of the most fearsome and fascinating creatures that roam the ocean's depths.

Topic: Severe Weather

Definition/Introduction

- ### *What is the topic? What does it cover?*

   Weather is the state of the atmosphere at a given time and place, with respect to variables such as temperature, moisture, wind velocity, and barometric pressure. Students study severe weather—its causes, conditions and effects to better understand and prepare. Severe weather includes hurricanes, tornadoes, blizzards, etc.

- ### *Catalog Subject Headings or Keywords*

   Weather
   Climatology
   Meteorology
   See also specific weather subjects, e.g. hurricanes.

- ### *Dewey Numbers*

   551.5 Meteorology
   551.6 Climatology and weather

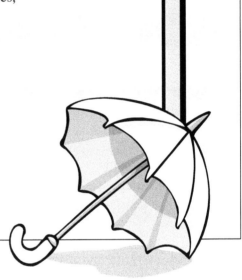

Print Resources

- ### *Reference titles [dictionaries, encyclopedias, atlases, specific subject references]*

   Allaby, Michael. *Encyclopedia of Weather and Climate.* Facts On File, c2002.

   Engelbert, Phillis. *The Complete Weather Resource.* UXL, c1997.

   The Facts On File Dictionary of Weather and Climate. Facts On File, c2001.

   Stein, Paul. *The Macmillan Encyclopedia of Weather.* Macmillan Reference USA, c2001.

   Weather and Climate On File. Facts On File, c2001.

- ### *General titles [nonfiction, any suitable fiction]*

   Be sure to check the library online catalog to find additional suitable materials.

   Allen, Jean. *Blizzards.* Capstone High-Interest Books, c2002.

   Friend, Sandra. *Earth's Wild Winds.* Twenty-First Century Books, c2002.

   Sakany, Lois. *Hurricane Hunters and Tornado Chasers: Life in the Eye of the Storm.* Rosen Central, 2003.

   Silverstein, Alvin. *Weather and Climate.* Twenty-First Century Books, c1998.

   Tsunamis. Greenhaven Press, Thomson/Gale, c2003.

■ *Journals*

Be sure to check any online periodical database at your school library for more.

Alpert, Mark. "Stormy Weather". *Scientific American*, Dec2004, Vol. 291 Issue 6, p28, 1p, 1c

Breslau, Karen. "A Hiker's Nightmare". *Newsweek*, 11/1/2004, Vol. 144 Issue 18, p30, 2/3p, 1c

Husick, Chuch. "Freak Weather: What Caused It?" *MotorBoating*, Dec2004, Vol. 194 Issue 6, p76, 1/2p, 1 map

"Some Notable Hurricanes, Typhoons, Blizzards, Other Storms". *World Almanac & Book of Facts*, 2004, p188, 2p, 1 chart

Web Resources

FEMA For Kids: The Disaster Area
http:// www.fema.gov/kids/dizarea.htm
"Although disasters themselves aren't fun, learning about them is!"

Hurricane and Natural Disaster Brochures
http://www.aoml.noaa.gov/general/lib/hurricbro.html
Includes fact sheets regarding a variety of natural disasters.

National Hurricane Center
http://www.nhc.noaa.gov
Learn about the hazards of hurricanes and what you can do to help protect yourself, your family, and your property.

The National Severe Storms Laboratory
http://www.nssl.noaa.gov/
"The people of NSSL, in partnership with the National Weather Service, are dedicated to improving severe weather warnings and forecasts in order to save lives and reduce property damage."

Storm Prediction Center (SPC)
http://www.spc.noaa.gov/index.shtml
Latest severe weather outlooks, watches, severe weather statistics, and historical severe weather data.

Topic: Tornadoes

Definition/Introduction

- ### *What is the topic? What does it cover?*

  Tornadoes are extremely violent revolving storms with swirling, funnel-shaped clouds caused by a rising column of warm air propelled by a strong wind. These storms have the potential for causing great destruction and loss of life.

- ### *Catalog Subject Headings or Keywords*

  Tornadoes
  Meteorology
  Storms
  Wind

- ### *Dewey Numbers*

  551.55 Tornadoes

Print Resources

- ### *Reference titles [dictionaries, encyclopedias, atlases, specific subject references]*

  Allaby, Michael. *Encyclopedia of Weather and Climate.* Facts On File, c2002.

  Engelbert, Phillis. *Dangerous Planet: The Science of Natural Disasters.* UXL, c2001.

  History's Most Devastating Disasters. Macmillan Reference USA, c2001.

  Stein, Paul. *The Macmillan Encyclopedia of Weather.* Macmillan Reference USA, 2001.

- ### *General titles [nonfiction, any suitable fiction]*

  Be sure to check the library online catalog to find additional suitable materials.

  Challoner, Jack. *Hurricane & Tornado.* DK Publishing, c2004.

  Engelbert, Phillis. *Dangerous Planet: The Science of Natural Disasters.* UXL, c2001.

  Galiano, Dean. *Tornadoes.* Rosen Central, c2000.

  Oxlade, Chris. *Storm Warning: Tornadoes.* Raintree, c2005.

  Sakany, Lois. *Hurricane Hunters and Tornado Chasers: Life in the Eye of the Storm.* Rosen Central, 2003.

  Scavuzzo, Wendy. *Tornado Alert!* Crabtree, c2004.

  White, Matt. *Storm Chasers: On the Trail of Deadly Tornadoes.* Capstone Curriculum Pub., c2003.

■ *Journals*

Be sure to check any online periodical database at your school library for more.

Chiang, Mona. "Alarming Twisters". (cover story) *Science World*, 9/20/2004, Vol. 61 Issue 2, p10, 4p, 2c, 1bw

"Tornado Safety Rules". *Children's Digest*, May/Jun2004, Vol. 54 Issue 3, p8, 1p

"Tornadoes 2004 Another Record-Setting Year". *Weatherwise*, Mar/Apr2005, Vol. 58 Issue 2, p44, 8p

Weir, Kirsten. "Mister Twister". (cover story) *Current Science*, 4/16/2004, Vol. 89 Issue 15, p4, 2p, 7c

Web Resources

FEMA for Kids – Tornadoes
http://www.fema.gov/kids/tornado.htm
Information about tornadoes and links to pictures and stories about their impact.

Fujita Tornado Damage Scale
http://www.spc.noaa.gov/faq/tornado/f-scale.html
A guide to the classification of tornadoes and what damage each is capable of.

National Oceanic and Atmospheric Administration
http://www.noaa.gov/tornadoes.html
Information about tornadoes including what to do if you are near one and how to prepare yourself for one.

National Weather Service
http://www.crh.noaa.gov/mkx/owlie/tornado1.htm
Would you know what to do if a tornado struck? This informative site gives you several scenarios and lets you know what to do in case of an emergency.

The Online Tornado FAQ
http://www.spc.noaa.gov/faq/tornado/
The Tornado FAQ is not intended to be a comprehensive guide to tornadoes. Instead, it is a quick-reference summary of tornado knowledge, which will link you to more detailed information.

Tornadoes – Nature's Most Violent Storms
http://www.nssl.noaa.gov/NWSTornado/
This preparedness guide includes safety information for schools.

Topic: Volcanoes

Definition/Introduction

■ *What is the topic? What does it cover?*

Volcanoes are a vent in the earth's crust from which molten rock, lava, ashes, and gases are ejected from beneath the surface.

■ *Catalog Subject Headings or Keywords*

Volcanoes
Geology
Mountains
Physical geography
    See also names of specific volcanoes.

■ *Dewey Numbers*

551.21 Volcanoes

Print Resources

■ *Reference titles [dictionaries, encyclopedias, atlases, specific subject references]*

Engelbert, Phillis. *Dangerous Planet: The Science of Natural Disasters.* UXL, c2001.

Nagel, Rob. *UXL Encyclopedia of Landforms and Other Geologic Features.* UXL, Thomson/Gale, c2004.

Oldershaw, Cally. *Atlas of Geology and Landforms.* Franklin Watts, c2001.

The Oxford Essential Geographical Dictionary. Berkley Books, c1999.

Ritchie, David. *Encyclopedia of Earthquakes and Volcanoes.* Facts On File, c2001.

■ *General titles [nonfiction, any suitable fiction]*

Be sure to check the library online catalog to find additional suitable materials.

Ball, Jacqueline A. *Volcanoes.* G. Stevens Pub., c2004.

Bredeson, Carmen. *Mount St. Helens Volcano: Violent Eruption.* Enslow Publishers, c2001.

Challen, Paul C. *Volcano Alert!* Crabtree, c2004.

Lassieur, Allison. *Volcanoes.* Capstone Books, c2001.

Lindop, Laurie. *Probing Volcanoes.* Twenty-First Century Books, c2003.

Van Rose, Susanna. *Volcano & Earthquake.* DK Publishing, c2004.

■ *Journals*

Be sure to check any online periodical database at your school library for more.

Perkins, Sid. "When Mountains Fizz". (cover story) *Science News*, 1/29/2005, Vol. 167 Issue 5, p74, 3p, 5c

Skelton, Renee. "Volcano!" *National Geographic Kids*, Dec2003 Issue 336, p20, 2p, 1c

Svitil, Kathy A. "Keeping an Eye on an Awakening Giant". *Discover*, Mar2005, Vol. 26 Issue 3, p13, 1/2p, 1c

"Undersea Volcano Viewed". *News for You*, 7/28/2004, Vol. 52 Issue 30, p2, 1/2p, 1 map, 2c

Web Resources

Cascades Volcano Observatory
http://vulcan.wr.usgs.gov/
Updates on Mount St. Helens and other Cascade Range volcanoes.

Electronic Volcano
http://www.dartmouth.edu/~volcano/
The Electronic Volcano is a window into the world of information on active volcanoes.

Global Volcanism Program
http://www.volcano.si.edu/
The Smithsonian's Global Volcanism Program seeks better understanding of all volcanoes through documenting their eruptions—small and large—during the past 10,000 years.

National Geographic Forces of Nature
http://www.nationalgeographic.com/forcesofnature/
Companion Web site to the movie "Forces of Nature." Discusses hurricanes, earthquakes, volcanoes, and tornadoes.

University of North Dakota Volcano World
http://volcano.und.nodak.edu/
"The web's premier source of volcano info."

Topic: Animals

Middle School Library Pathfinder

Pathfinders are guides which are intended to help you get started doing research on a particular topic, both online and at your library. Although these resources are useful as a starting point for your research, they are not the only resources that are available to you.

Definition/Introduction

- ### *What is the topic? What does it cover?*

  There are many types of animals living in the world. They come in all shapes and sizes and live in many different climates. In this unit, we will study a variety of different animals and learn about their lives.

- ### *Catalog Subject Headings or Keywords*

  Animals

  See also names of specific animals or animal families.

- ### *Dewey Numbers*

  590s Animals
  636 Animal husbandry

Print Resources

- ### *Reference titles [dictionaries, encyclopedias, atlases, specific subject references]*

  Animal Anatomy On File. Facts On File, c2003.

  Benson, Sonia. *Endangered Species.* UXL, Thomson/Gale, c2004.

  Johnson, Jinny. *National Geographic Animal Encyclopedia.* National Geographic Society, c2000.

  Kerrod, Robin. *Facts On File Wildlife Atlas.* Facts On File, c1997.

  UXL Encyclopedia of Biomes. UXL, c2000.

- ### *General titles [nonfiction, any suitable fiction]*

  Be sure to check the library online catalog to find additional suitable materials.

  Dalgleish, Sharon. *Protecting Wildlife.* Chelsea House, c2003.

  Pringle, Laurence P. *Strange Animals, New to Science.* Marshall Cavendish, c2002.

  Stonehouse, Bernard. *How Animals Live: The Amazing World of Animals in the Wild.* Scholastic Reference, c2004.

  Thomas, Peggy. *Marine Mammal Preservation.* Twenty-First Century Books, c2000.

  Whyman, Kathryn. *The Animal Kingdom: A Guide to Vertebrate Classification and Biodiversity.* Raintree Steck-Vaughn, c2000.

  The Young Oxford Library of Science. Oxford University Press, c2002, c2001.

- ## *Journals*

Be sure to check any online periodical database at your school library for more.

Heyman, J.D., et al. "Danger in the Backyard". *People*, 7/12/2004, Vol. 62 Issue 2, p97, 4p, 10c, 1bw

Tangley, Laura. "News of the Wild". *National Wildlife*, Oct/Nov2003, Vol. 41 Issue 6, p8, 1p, 2c

Williams, Ted. "Earth Almanac". *Audubon*, Mar/Apr99, Vol. 101 Issue 2, p126, 2p, 6c

Web Resources

Animal Diversity Web
http://animaldiversity.ummz.umich.edu/site/index.html
Diversity Web (ADW) is an online database of animal natural history, distribution, classification, and conservation biology at the University of Michigan.

Science & Nature: Animals
http://www.bbc.co.uk/nature/animals/
Maintained by the BBC, this site has lots of information about many kids of animals.

Museum of Nature
http://www.nature.ca/notebooks/english/mon2.htm
On this site, you'll find lots of fascinating facts about 246 animal species.

The Electronic Zoo
http://netvet.wustl.edu/e-zoo.htm
Information about animals in an easy-to-use format.

Kratts' Creatures
http://www.pbs.org/kratts/
Explore the fascinating and funny creatures of the world over.

National Geographic Creature Feature
http://www.nationalgeographic.com/kids/creature_feature/archive/
"Get to know some of the most interesting and unusual members of the wild world—from cheetahs to crocodiles and whales to warthogs. Dive in for photos, video, audio, postcards, fun facts, and more!"

Topic: Biomes

Definition/Introduction

- *What is the topic? What does it cover?*

  A biome is a distinct, natural community chiefly distinguished by its plant life and climate.

- *Catalog Subject Headings or Keywords*

  Biomes
  Biotic communities
  Ecology
  Ecosystems
  > *See also sub category topics such as: coniferous forest, deciduous forest, desert, grassland, lake and pond, ocean, rainforest, river and stream, seashore, tundra, and wetland.*

- *Dewey Numbers*

  577 Ecology

Print Resources

- *Reference titles [dictionaries, encyclopedias, atlases, specific subject references]*

  Biomes Atlases. Raintree Steck-Vaughn, c2003, c2002.

  UXL Encyclopedia of Biomes. UXL, c2000.

  Whitfield, Philip. *Biomes and Habitats.* Macmillan Reference USA, Gale Group/Thomson Learning, 2002.

- *General titles [nonfiction, any suitable fiction]*

  Be sure to check the library online catalog to find additional suitable materials.

  Tocci, Salvatore. *Alpine Tundra (Watts Library—Biomes and Habitats).* Franklin Watts, c2005.

  Tocci, Salvatore. *Arctic Tundra (Watts Library—Biomes and Habitats).* Franklin Watts, c2005.

  Tocci, Salvatore *The Chaparral Life on the Scrubby Coast (Watts Library—Biomes and Habitats).* Franklin Watts, c2005.

  Tocci, Salvatore. *Coral Reefs Life Below the Sea (Watts Library—Biomes and Habitats).* Franklin Watts, c2005.

  Tocci, Salvatore. *Marine Habitats Life in Saltwater (Watts Library—Biomes and Habitats).* Franklin Watts, c2005.

  Toupin, Laurie Peach. *Life in the Temperate Grasslands (Watts Library—Biomes and Habitats).* Franklin Watts, c2005.

Toupin, Laurie Peach. *Savannas—Life in the Tropical Grasslands (Watts Library—Biomes and Habitats)*. Franklin Watts, c2005.

■ Journals

Be sure to check any online periodical database at your school library for more.

"Look Around". *Kids Discover*, Feb2002, Vol. 12 Issue 2, p2, 2p, 2c

"Our World". *Kids Discover*, Feb2002, Vol. 12 Issue 2, p4, 2p, 1 map, 10c

Web Resources

Earth Observatory
http://earthobservatory.nasa.gov/Laboratory/Biome/
NASA site on which you can explore coniferous forests, temperate deciduous forests, deserts, grasslands, rainforests, shrub lands, and tundras.

Ecosystems – High School Environmental Center – U.S. EPA
http://www.epa.gov/highschool/ecosystems.htm
Learn about different ecosystems and strategies for restoring them, as well as the effects of pollution on this US Environmental Protection Agency site.

Global 200: Blueprint for a Living Planet – Major Habitat Types
http://www.panda.org/about_wwf/where_we_work/ecoregions/global200/pages/terra.htm
Developed by World Wildlife Foundation scientists in collaboration with experts around the world, provides a blueprint for biodiversity conservation on a global scale. It includes information on every major habitat type.

MBGnet – Biomes of the World
http://mbgnet.mobot.org/
This site, posted by the Missouri Botanical Garden, has information on definitions, types, causes, locations, plants, and animals for each type of biome.

Worldbiomes.com
http://www.worldbiomes.com
This site, selected by the SciLinks program, a service of National Science Teachers Association, covers major world biomes.

Topic: Endangered Species

Definition/Introduction

■ *What is the topic? What does it cover?*

Endangered species are those at risk of extinction through the destruction of all or a significant portion of their natural habitats. Threatened species are those that are likely to become endangered in the foreseeable future.

■ *Catalog Subject Headings or Keywords*

Endangered species
Nature conservation
Rare animals
Wildlife conservation
　　See also names of individual species.

■ *Dewey Numbers*

333.95　Biological resources
578.68　Rare and endangered species

Print Resources

■ *Reference titles [dictionaries, encyclopedias, atlases, specific subject references]*

Beacham's Guide to International Endangered Species. Beacham Pub., Gale Group, c2001, c1998.

Benson, Sonia. *Endangered Species.* UXL, Thomson/Gale, c2004.

UXL Encyclopedia of Biomes. UXL, c2000.

■ *General titles [nonfiction, any suitable fiction]*

Be sure to check the library online catalog to find additional suitable materials.

Hoff, Mary King. *Our Endangered Planet. Life on Land.* Lerner Publications, c1992.

Miles, Victoria. *Wild Science: Amazing Encounters Between Animals and the People Who Study Them.* Raincoast Books, Publishers Group West, c2004.

Whitman, Sylvia. *This Land Is Your Land: The American Conservation Movement.* Lerner Publications, c1994.

■ *Journals*

Be sure to check any online periodical database at your school library for more.

"Countries with the Most Threatened Species". *Weekly Reader—Senior*, 10/15/2004, Vol. 83 Issue 6, p8, 1/4p

Ridgley, Heidi. "Left Off Our List". *National Wildlife*, Aug/Sep2004, Vol. 42 Issue 5, P46, 1/4p, 1c

"Warning: Animals At Risk". *Time for Kids*, 4/23/2004 World Edition, Vol. 9 Issue 24, p2, 2p, 3c

Weir, Kirsten. "Born To Be Wild". (cover story) *Current Science*, 1/7/2005, Vol. 90 Issue 9, p4, 2p, 6c

"Will We Save the Prairie Dog From Extinction?" *E Magazine: The Environmental Magazine*, Sep/Oct2004, Vol. 15 Issue 5, p13, 1p, 1bw

Web Resources

Endangered Specie.com
http://www.endangeredspecie.com/
Information about the causes of endangerment, the reasons for actions, and ways to help.

Wildlife Federation
http://www.nwf.org/wildlifeuniversity/endangered.cfm
Information about wildlife and the events that threaten them.

Threatened and Endangered Species System (TESS)
http://ecos.fws.gov/tess_public/TESSUsmap?status=listed
Click on a state to get a listing of endangered species and information about them.

Threatened Animals of the World Database
http://www.unep-wcmc.org/index.html?http://quin.unep-wcmc.org/isdb/taxonomy/~main
The database is searchable by country and species.

Turner Endangered Species Fund
http://tesf.org/tesf/links/
Conservation links.

U.S. Fish and Wildlife Service
http://endangered.fws.gov/
Working together for endangered species recovery.

World Wildlife Fund
http://www.worldwildlife.org/endangered/index.cfm
Endangered Wildlife page with links to animals in danger.

Topic: Food Chain

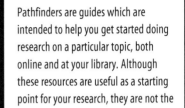

Definition/Introduction

- ### What is the topic? What does it cover?

  The food chain is the sequence of organisms through which energy and other nutrients are transferred. Some animals eat plants. In turn, other animals eat these animals. The other animals may eat them, and so on.

- ### Catalog Subject Headings or Keywords

  Food chain (ecology)
  Food web
  Animals – Food
  Ecology

- ### Dewey Numbers

  577 Ecology

Print Resources

- ### Reference titles [dictionaries, encyclopedias, atlases, specific subject references]

  Knight, Judson. *Science of Everyday Things. Volume 3, Real-Life Biology.* Thomson/Gale, c2002.

  UXL Encyclopedia of Biomes. UXL, c2000.

- ### General titles [nonfiction, any suitable fiction]

  Be sure to check the library online catalog to find additional suitable materials.

  Ganeri, Anita. *Food Chains.* Heinemann Library, c2004.

  Greenaway, Theresa. *Food Chains.* Raintree Steck-Vaughn, c2001, c2000.

  Nadeau, Isaac. *Food Chains in a Pond Habitat.* PowerKids Press, c2002.

  Silverstein, Alvin. *Food Chains.* Twenty-First Century Books, c1998.

  Spilsbury, Louise. *Food Chains and Webs: From Producers to Decomposers.* Heinemann Library, c2004.

- ### Journals

  Be sure to check any online periodical database at your school library for more.

  "A Food Chain". *Kids Discover*, Mar2004, Vol. 14 Issue 3, p6, 1/3p, 13c

  Hayden, Thomas. "Trashing the Oceans". *U.S. News & World Report*, 11/4/2002, Vol. 133 Issue 17, p58, 3p, 1 map, 3c

"Rain Forest Food Web". *Kids Discover*, Jun/Jul95, Vol. 5 Issue 6, p4, 2p, 1 diagram

"Who's Eating Whom?" *Kids Discover*, Feb2002, Vol. 12 Issue 2, p6, 1p

Web Resources

Food Chains
http://users.rcn.com/jkimball.ma.ultranet/BiologyPages/F/FoodChains.html
Explains the energy flow through food chains.

Food Chains and Webs
http://www.vtaide.com/png/foodchains.htm
Information about the food chain and a chance to create your own.

Food Web
http://oceanlink.island.net/oinfo/foodweb/foodweb.html
The food web in the ocean is diagramed.

PhysicalGeography.net
http://www.physicalgeography.net/fundamentals/4e.html
Explains the food chain as an example of a system.

PlanetPals
http://www.planetpals.com/foodchain.html
Plenty of kid-friendly information on the food chain.

Topic: Invasive Species

Definition/Introduction

■ *What is the topic? What does it cover?*

Invasive species are non-indigenous species that have evolved elsewhere and have been relocated and are now upsetting the ecological balance. These species may have been purposely or accidentally relocated from their original habitat.

■ *Catalog Subject Headings or Keywords*

Alien plants
Aquatic pests
Biological invasion
Invasive plants
Invasive species
Non-indigenous pests
Pest introduction
Plant invasions

■ *Dewey Numbers*

363.7 Environmental problems
581.6 Miscellaneous nontaxomic kinds of plants
577 Ecology

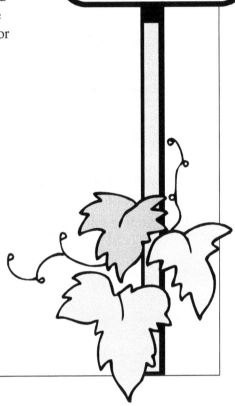

Print Resources

■ *Reference titles [dictionaries, encyclopedias, atlases, specific subject references]*

Ashworth, William. *Encyclopedia of Environmental Studies*. Facts On File, c2001.

Junior Environment On File. Facts On File, c1997.

Kerrod, Robin. *Facts On File Wildlife Atlas*. Facts On File, c1997.

Souza, D.M. *Plant Invaders*. Franklin Watts, c2003.

■ *General titles [nonfiction, any suitable fiction]*

Be sure to check the library online catalog to find additional suitable materials.

"Below The Surface, The Great Lakes Are Suffering From Ecosystem Shock". *National Wildlife*, Dec2004/Jan2005, Vol. 43 Issue 1, p64, 1p, 1c

Dougherty, Ryan. "Invasive Fern Smothers Plants". *National Parks*, May/Jun2003, Vol. 77 Issue 5/6, p12, 2p, 1c

Schweiger, Larry J. "A Global Trade Agreement Must Address Invasive Species". *National Wildlife*, Oct/Nov2004, Vol. 42 Issue 6, p9, 2/3p

Smith, Steph. "Fish Out of Water". *Scholastic News*—Senior Edition, 9/13/2002, Vol. 71 Issue 2, p6, 1p, 1 map, 2c

Warrick, Joby. "A River Once Ran Through It". *National Wildlife*, Feb2002, Vol. 40 Issue 2, p32, 6p, 1 map, 3c

Web Resources

Federal Noxious Weed List
http://plants.usda.gov/cgi_bin/topics.cgi?earl=noxious.cgi
List searchable by species and location.

Invaders Database System
http://invader.dbs.umt.edu/
The INVADERS Database is a comprehensive database of exotic plant names and weed distribution records for five states in the northwestern United States.

Invasive Species Initiative
http://tncweeds.ucdavis.edu/index.html
The Invasive Species Initiative is The Nature Conservancy's response to abating the damage caused to native biodiversity by the human-facilitated introduction of non-native, harmful invasive species. This web site provides many resources designed to help all conservationists deal most effectively with invasive species.

Invasivespecies.gov
http://www.invasivespecies.gov/.gov
Invasivespecies.gov the gateway to federal efforts concerning invasive species.

Non-native Invasive Plants of the Midwest and Eastern United States
http://www.easywildflowers.com/invasive.htm
A listing of non-native species.

Weeds Gone Wild
http://www.nps.gov/plants/alien/
Alien plant invaders of natural areas is a Web-based project of the Plant Conservation Alliance's Alien Plant Working Group, which provides information for the general public.

Topic: Nutrition

Definition/Introduction

- ### *What is the topic? What does it cover?*

    This topic covers the study of nutrition from coverage of what makes up a balanced diet to the adverse effects of an inadequate diet.

- ### *Catalog Subject Headings or Keywords*

    Nutrition
    Food
    Diet
    Digestion

- ### *Dewey Numbers*

    613.2 Dietetics

Print Resources

- ### *Reference titles [dictionaries, encyclopedias, atlases, specific subject references]*

    Applegate, Elizabeth Ann. *Encyclopedia of Sports & Fitness Nutrition*. Prima Pub., c2002.

    Encyclopedia of Human Nutrition. Academic Press, c1999.

    Health On File. Facts On File, c2002.

    Levchuck, Caroline M. *Healthy Living*. UXL, c2000.

    Macmillan Health Encyclopedia. Macmillan Reference USA, c1999.

- ### *General titles [nonfiction, any suitable fiction]*

    Be sure to check the library online catalog to find additional suitable materials.

    Bickerstaff, Linda. *Nutrition Sense—Counting Calories Figuring Out Fats, and Eating Balanced Meals (The Library Of Nutrition)* Rosen Pub. Group, c2004.

    Cheung, Lillian Wai-Yin. *Be Healthy! It's A Girl Thing: Food, Fitness, and Feeling Great*. Crown, c2003.

    Landau, Elaine. *A Healthy Diet*. Franklin Watts, c2003.

    McCarthy, Rose. *Food Labels—Using Nutrition Information to Create a Healthy Diet (The Library of Nutrition)* Rosen Pub. Group, c2005.

    Silate, Jennifer. *Planning and Preparing Healthy Meals and Snacks—A Day-To-Day Guide to a Healthier Diet (The Library of Nutrition)*. Rosen Pub. Group, c2005.

Tecco, Betsy Dru. *Food For Fuel—The Connection Between Food and Physical Activity (The Library of Nutrition)*. Rosen Pub. Group, c2004.

■ *Journals*

Be sure to check any online periodical database at your school library for more.

Healy, Bernadine. "Rebuilding the Pyramid". *U.S. News & World Report*, 9/6/2004, Vol. 137 Issue 7, p84, 1p, 1c, 1bw

Kuchment, Anna. "A Tough Balancing Act". *Newsweek*, 2/21/2005, Vol. 145 Issue 8, p61, 2p, 1c

Miller, Jeanne. "Rebuilding the Food Pyramid". *Odyssey*, May2004, Vol. 13 Issue 5, p16, 5p, 2 diagrams, 3c

"Should Soda Be Banned From School?" *Junior Scholastic*, 1/10/2004, Vol. 107 Issue 10, p5, 1p, 1 cartoon

Woods, Mark. "You Are What You Eat". *Boys' Life*, Feb2005, Vol. 95 Issue 2, p24, 4p, 1c

Web Resources

American Dietetic Association: Food and Nutrition Information
http://www.eatright.org/Public/NutritionInformation/92.cfm
ADA is your link to reliable, objective food and nutrition information. The resources will help you achieve a healthy lifestyle and answer your food and nutrition questions.

Grains Nutrition Information Center
http://www.wheatfoods.org/
Learn the important role grains play in planning a sensible eating plan.

MayoClinic: Nutrition Center
http://www.mayoclinic.com/findinformation/healthylivingcenter/centers.cfm?objectid=000851DA-6222-1B37-8D7E80C8D77A0000
Updated daily, this site is a great place to check major developments related to nutrition.

Vegetarian Resource Group
http://www.vrg.org/
Five million adults in the United States are vegetarians. This site guides you towards staying healthy as a vegetarian.

Topic: Rainforests

Middle School Library Pathfinder

Pathfinders are guides which are intended to help you get started doing research on a particular topic, both online and at your library. Although these resources are useful as a starting point for your research, they are not the only resources that are available to you.

Definition/Introduction

■ *What is the topic? What does it cover?*

The rainforest is a dense evergreen forest occupying a tropical region with an annual rainfall of at least 100 inches.

■ *Catalog Subject Headings or Keywords*

Rainforest or rain forest
Biodiversity
Jungle
Ecosystem
Tropical
Deforestation
Climate

■ *Dewey Numbers*

577.34 Rain forest ecology
634.9 Forestry
910 Geography
333.7 Land economics

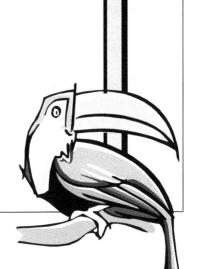

Print Resources

■ *Reference titles [dictionaries, encyclopedias, atlases, specific subject references]*

The Encyclopedia of the Environment. Franklin Watts, c1999.

Junior Environment On File. Facts On File, c1997.

UXL Encyclopedia of Biomes. UXL, c2000.

■ *General titles [nonfiction, any suitable fiction]*

Be sure to check the library online catalog to find additional suitable materials.

Dalgleish, Sharon. *Protecting Forests.* Chelsea House, c2003.

Green, Jen. *Rain Forest Revealed* DK Publishing, c2004.

Jackson, Tom. *Tropical Forests.* Raintree Steck-Vaughn, c2003.

McLeish, Ewan. *Rain Forests: Our Impact on the Planet.* Raintree Steck-Vaughn, c2002.

Welsbacher, Anne. *Life in a Rain Forest.* Lerner Publications, c2003.

■ *Journals*

Be sure to check any online periodical database at your school library for more.

De Seve, Karen. "Welcome To My Jungle.. Before It's Gone". *Science World*, 3/11/2002, Vol. 58 Issue 11, p7, 5p, 8c

"Habitats Are Homes". *Science Spin—Early Primary*, Apr2004, p2, 2p, 5c

Hardman, Chris. "Forests on a Fast Track Forward". Americas, Sep/Oct2004, Vol. 56 Issue 5, p3, 2p, 1c

"Rain Forests". *Junior Scholastic*, 4/8/2002, Vol. 104 Issue 16, p11, 1/2p, 1c

Web Resources

Biomes of the World: Rainforest
http://mbgnet.mobot.org/sets/rforest/index.htm
Information and pictures of tropical rainforests.

Tropical Rainforest
http://www.blueplanetbiomes.org/rainforest.htm
Information about the plants, animals, and climate of tropical rainforests.

Welcome to the Rainforest
http://rain-tree.com/
Information about the possible medicinal uses of the rainforest plants.

The World's Rainforests
http://www.nafi.com.au/faq/index.php3?fact=14
Information about the causes of deforestation and the efforts to save the rainforests.

Topic: Science Fair Projects

Definition/Introduction

■ *What is the topic? What does it cover?*

In many schools, students demonstrate their understanding of the scientific process by preparing and carrying out a science experiment. These may or may not be entered into a competition. Here you will find resources for completing a successful science fair project.

■ *Catalog Subject Headings or Keywords*

Science projects
Science – Experiments
Science – Exhibitions
Science fairs

■ *Dewey Numbers*

507 Science education

Print Resources

■ *Reference titles [dictionaries, encyclopedias, atlases, specific subject references]*

Be sure to check the library online catalog to find additional suitable materials

Barrow, Lloyd H. *Science Fair Projects Investigating Earthworms.* Enslow Publishers, c2000.

Gardner, Robert. *Science Projects about Light.* Enslow Publishers, c1994.

Gardner, Robert. *Science Projects about Math.* Enslow Publishers, c1999.

Gardner, Robert. *Science Projects about Physics in the Home.* Enslow Publishers, c1999.

Gardner, Robert. *Science Projects about Plants.* Enslow Publishers, c1999.

Gardner, Robert. *Science Projects about the Environment and Ecology.* Enslow Publishers, c1999.

Haduch, Bill. *Science Fair Success Secrets: How to Win Prizes, Have Fun, and Think Like a Scientist.* Dutton Children's Books, c2002.

Rybolt, Thomas R. *Environmental Experiments about Renewable Energy.* Enslow Publishers, c1994.

VanCleave, Janice Pratt. *Janice VanCleave's A+ Projects in Astronomy: Winning Experiments for Science Fairs and Extra Credit.* John Wiley, c2002.

VanCleave, Janice Pratt. *Janice VanCleave's A+ Projects in Biology: Winning Experiments for Science Fairs and Extra Credit.* John Wiley, c1993.

VanCleave, Janice Pratt. *Janice VanCleave's A+ Projects in Chemistry: Winning Experiments for Science Fairs and Extra Credit.* John Wiley, c1993.

VanCleave, Janice Pratt. *Janice VanCleave's A+ Projects in Earth Science: Winning Experiments for Science Fairs and Extra Credit*. John Wiley, c1999.

VanCleave, Janice Pratt. *Janice VanCleave's A+ Projects in Physics: Winning Experiments for Science Fairs and Extra Credit*. John Wiley, c2003.

■ *Journals*

Be sure to check any online periodical database at your school library for more.

Chiles, James R. "At Science Fairs There's Not Much Playing Around". *Smithsonian*, Sep90, Vol. 21 Issue 6, p62, 9p, 12c

West, Krista. "Science Fair Success". *Scientific American Explorations*, Winter2001, Vol. 4 Issue 1, p38, 3p

Web Resources

Discovery School Science Fair Central
http:://school.discovery.com/sciencefaircentral/
A comprehensive guide to creating your science fair project!

Internet Public Library Science Fair Project Resource Guide
http://www.ipl.org/div/kidspace/projectguide/
The IPL will guide you to a variety of Web site resources, leading you through the necessary steps to successfully complete a science experiment.

Preparing a Science Fair Project
http://www.swlauriersb.qc.ca/endlish/edservices/pedresources/webquest/sciwq.htm
Looking for a topic that you can use in this year's Science Fair? Don't quite know how to get started? In this WebQuest, you will learn how to prepare and carry out a project that will be fun and interesting.

Science Fair Project Ideas
http://sciencefairproject.virtualave.net/l
Online store for all things science!

The Ultimate Science Fair Resource
http:://www.scifair.org/.org
Scifair.org is the premiere resource for help with science fair projects, science fair ideas, tips on carrying out science experiments, and creating winning science fair projects.

Mathematics

Topic: Fractals

Definition/Introduction

- ### *What is the topic? What does it cover?*

  Fractals are irregular shapes on a surface produced by a procedure or repeated subdivision.

- ### *Catalog Subject Headings or Keywords*

  Fractals
  Fractal geometry
  Geometry
  Topology

- ### *Dewey Numbers*

  514 Topology

Print Resources

- ### *General titles [nonfiction, any suitable fiction]*

  Be sure to check the library online catalog to find additional suitable materials.

  Feder, Jens. *Fractals*. Plenum Press, c1988.

  Hilton, Peter John. *Mathematical Reflections: In a Room With Many Mirrors*. Springer, c1997.

  Mandelbrot, Benoit B. *The Fractal Geometry of Nature*. W.H. Freeman, c1983.

  Pappas, Theoni. *Fractals, Googols, and Other Mathematical Tales*. Wide World Pub./Tetra, c1993.

  Peterson, Ivars. *Math Trek: Adventures in the Mathzone*. John Wiley, c2000.

- ### *Journals*

  Be sure to check any online periodical database at your school library for more.

  "Fractals: Painting by Numbers". *World Almanac for Kids*, 2005, p184, 1/3p

  Perkins, Sid. "It's a Rough World". Science News, 2/2/2002, Vol. 161 Issue 5, p75, 2p, 2c

  Peterson, Ivars. "Fractal Past, Fractal Future". *Science News*, 03/01/97, Vol. 151 Issue 9, pS13, 1p, 1c

  Peterson, Ivars. "Fractured Granite and Fractal Prints". *Math Trek*, Apr2003, pN.PAG, 00p

Web Resources

Exploring Fractals
http://www.math.umass.edu/~mconnors/fractal/fractal.html
This World Wide Web project commenced in July 1994. It is based on a curriculum, entitled "Exploring Fractal Dimension," developed by Mary Ann Connors and Anna Rose Haralampus at an NSF funded Institute for High School Mathematics Teachers at Georgetown University July - August, 1991. A wonderful site with great general fractal information.

Fractalism
http://www.mathematicimages.com/
Jay Jacobson's latest fractal art.

Fractal Links
http://www.fractal.org/Bewustzijns-Besturings-Model/Fractal-Links.htm
Links to fractal information online.

Fractal Music
http://thinks.com/webguide/fractal-music.htm
Lots of links to fractal music.

Fractal Pictures
http://www.jracademy.com/~jtucek/math/picts.html
This site contains many interesting pictures of fractals.

A Fractals Unit for Elementary and Middle School Students
http://math.rice.edu/~lanius/frac/
Middle school level fractal information and pictures.

The Fractory
http://library.thinkquest.org/3288/
This page will help you learn about fractals: what they are and how to design them, but it will also let you discover more on your own.

Intro to Fractals
http://astronomy.swin.edu.au/~pbourke/fractals/fracintro/
This is a good place to start for fractal information.

The Spanky Fractal Database
http://spanky.triumf.ca/
This is a collection of fractals and fractal related material for free distribution on the net. Most of the software was gathered from various ftp sites on the Internet and it is generally freeware or shareware.

Topic: Mathematicians

Definition/Introduction

■ *What is the topic? What does it cover?*

You will be researching a mathematician and will learn about the person's life and contributions to the field of mathematics.

■ *Catalog Subject Headings or Keywords*

Mathematicians
> *See also names of individual mathematicians.*

■ *Dewey Numbers*

510 Mathematics

Print Resources

■ *Reference titles [dictionaries, encyclopedias, atlases, specific subject references]*

Mathematicians and Computer Wizards. Macmillan Reference USA, c2001.

McElroy, Tucker. *A to Z of Mathematicians*. Facts On File, c2005.

Notable Mathematicians: From Ancient Times to the Present. Gale Research, c1998.

Notable Women in Mathematics: A Biographical Dictionary. Greenwood Press, 1998.

Yount, Lisa. *A to Z of Women in Science and Math*. Facts On File, c1999.

■ *General titles [nonfiction, any suitable fiction]*

Be sure to check the library online catalog to find additional suitable materials.

Henderson, Harry. *Modern Mathematicians*. Facts On File, c1996.

Perl, Teri. *Women and Numbers: Lives of Women Mathematicians Plus Discovery Activities*. Wide World Publishing/Tetra, c1993.

Reimer, Luetta. *Mathematicians Are People, Too: Stories From the Lives of Great Mathematicians*. Dale Seymour Publications, c1990.

Reimer, Luetta. *Mathematicians Are People, Too: Stories From the Lives of Great Mathematicians: Volume 2*. Dale Seymour Publications, c1995.

■ *Journals*

Be sure to check any online periodical database at your school library for more. Try searching using the name of the mathematician you are researching.

Web Resources

Biographies of Women Mathematicians
http://www.agnesscott.edu/lriddle/women/women.htm
Part of an ongoing project by the students in mathematics at Agnes Scott College in Atlanta, Georgia.

Chronology of Mathematicians
http://www-groups.dcs.st-and.ac.uk/~history/Chronology/Chronology.html
A chronology of mathematicians between dates stated.

Faces of Science: African Americans in the Sciences
http://www.princeton.edu/~mcbrown/display/faces.html
Profiled here are African American men and women who have contributed to the advancement of science. Click on Mathematicians.

Famous Mathematicians
http://euler.ciens.ucv.ve/English/mathematics/
Biographies prepared by the Mathematics School, Central University of Venezuela.

History of Mathematics
http://aleph0.clarku.edu/~djoyce/mathhist/chronology.html
Chronological list of mathematicians.

Indexes of Biographies
http://www-gap.dcs.st-and.ac.uk/~history/BiogIndex.html
Alphabetical and chronological indexes. Site is maintained by the School of Mathematics and Statistics, University of St. Andrews, Scotland.

Mathematicians of the African Diaspora
http://www.math.buffalo.edu/mad/index.html
A Web site dedicated to the accomplishments of the peoples of Africa and the African Diaspora within the mathematical sciences.

Mathematicians of the Seventeenth and Eighteenth Centuries
http://www.maths.tcd.ie/pub/HistMath/People/RBallHist.html
"Available here are accounts of the lives and works of seventeenth and eighteenth century mathematicians (and some other scientists), adapted from *A Short Account of the History of Mathematics* by W. W. Rouse Ball (4th Edition, 1908)."

Muslim Scientists and Islamic Civilization
http://www.cyberistan.org/islamic/index.htm#biosc
Scientific contributions before the European Renaissance.

Topic: Tessellations

Definition/Introduction

■ *What is the topic? What does it cover?*

A tessellation is a careful positioning of shapes in a repeating pattern forming a mosaic pattern by using small shapes.

■ *Catalog Subject Headings or Keywords*

Tessellations (Mathematics)
Patterns (Mathematics)

■ *Dewey Numbers*

511 General principles of mathematics
516 Geometry
745.4 Art design

Print Resources

■ *Reference titles [dictionaries, encyclopedias, atlases, specific subject references]*

Check in general encyclopedias for basic information about tessellations.

■ *General titles [nonfiction, any suitable fiction]*

Be sure to check the library online catalog to find additional suitable materials.

Escher, M.C. *Escher On Escher: Exploring the Infinite.* Harry Abrams, c1989.

Escher, M.C. *The Magic of M.C. Escher.* Harry Abrams, c2000.

Kaleidoscopes, Hubcaps, and Mirrors: Symmetry and Transformations. Dale Seymour Publications, c1998.

Seymour, Dale. *Introduction to Tessellations.* Dale Seymour Publications, c1989.

Zaslavsky, Claudia. *More Math Games & Activities From Around the World.* Chicago Review Press, c2003.

■ *Journals*

Be sure to check any online periodical database at your school library for more.

"Monkeying Around with Art". *Zoobooks*, Jul95, Vol. 12 Issue 10, pB, 2p, 1bw

Peterson, Ivars. "Paper Folds, Creases, and Theorems". Science News, 1/21/95, Vol. 147 Issue 3, p44, 1/2p, 2 diagrams

Schattscheider, Doris. "The Tessellating World of M.C. Escher". Odyssey, Nov99, Vol. 8 Issue 8, p18, 3p

Wills, Steven R. "Tag Team Trials with the Tessellator Twins". *Odyssey*, Oct97, Vol. 6 Issue 7, p13, 3p, 1 cartoon

Web Resources

Coolmath.com
http://www.coolmath.com/tesspag1.htm
Information about tessellations and how to create them out of varying shapes.

Symmetry and Tessellations
http://ccins.camosun.bc.ca/~jbritton/jbsymteslk.htm
Activities to explore the concepts of symmetry and tessellations.

Tessellation Tutorials
http://mathforum.org/sum95/suzanne/tess.intro.html
Tutorials and templates for making your own tessellations.

Tessellations.org
http://www.tessellations.org/
Information about all aspects of tessellations.

Wonders of Math
http://www.math.com/students/wonders/tessellations.html
Links to various sites about tessellations.

Topic: Folklore and Folktales

Middle School Library Pathfinder

Pathfinders are guides which are intended to help you get started doing research on a particular topic, both online and at your library. Although these resources are useful as a starting point for your research, they are not the only resources that are available to you.

Definition/Introduction

- ### *What is the topic? What does it cover?*

  The roots of folklore stem from the oral tradition and culture of a people expressed in legends, riddles, songs, tales, and proverbs.

- ### *Catalog Subject Headings or Keywords*

  Folklore
  Legends
  Folktales

- ### *Dewey Numbers*

  398 Folklore

Print Resources

- ### *Reference titles [dictionaries, encyclopedias, atlases, specific subject references]*

  Favorite Folktales From Around the World. Pantheon Books, c1986.

  Folktales Told Around the World. University of Chicago Press, c1975.

  Mercatante, Anthony S. *The Facts On File Encyclopedia of World Mythology and Legend.* Facts On File, c2004.

  Pickering, David. *A Dictionary of Folklore.* Facts On File, c1999.

- ### *General titles [nonfiction, any suitable fiction]*

  Be sure to check the library online catalog to find additional suitable materials.

  DeSpain, Pleasant. *Eleven Turtle Tales: Adventure Tales From Around the World.* August House, c1994.

  Earth Care: World Folktales to Talk About. Linnet Books, c1999.

  Hamilton, Virginia. *In the Beginning: Creation Stories From Around the World.* Harcourt Brace Jovanovich, c1988.

  Spencer, Ann. *Song of the Sea: Myths, Tales, and Folklore.* Tundra Books, c2001.

  Stockings of Buttermilk: American Folktales. Clarion Books, c1999.

  Yep, Laurence. *The Rainbow People.* HarperTrophy, c1992, c1989.

■ *Journals*

Be sure to check any online periodical database at your school library for more.

"The Legend of Baba Yaga". *Time for Kids*, 3/5/2004 World Edition, Vol. 9 Issue 19, p8, 1/2p, 1c

Kissil, Don. "Folktale! Why Butterflies No Longer Sing". *Skipping Stones*, Mar/Apr2004, Vol. 16 Issue 2, p25, 2p, 1bw

Ross, Emma. "The Mighty Leopard". *Calliope*, Feb2005, Vol. 15 Issue 6, p34, 2p, 6c

Web Resources

Electronic Journal of Folklore
http://haldjas.folklore.ee/folklore/
Articles describe where different aspects of cultures came from and try to explain what the different folktales mean.

Encyclopedia Mythica
http://www.pantheon.org/
Information about tales and stories of the past from around the world.

Folklore and Mythology Electronic Texts
http://www.pitt.edu/~dash/folktexts.html
Online links to folktales and mythology listed on the Internet.

The Library of Congress: American Folklife Center
http://lcweb.loc.gov/folklife/afc.html
Information about folktales and folklore from American past.

Myths, Folktales and Fairy Tales
http://teacher.scholastic.com/writewit/mff/
There are activities for the students as well as information for the teachers on how to use this resource with their classes.

Stories Legends and Folktales from Around the World
http://www.unc.edu/~rwilkers/title.htm
Tales from different countries around the world.

The World & I: Worldwide Folktales
http://www.worldandi.com/wwft/demo.html
List of folktales from all over the world with full text documents.

Topic: Mythology

Middle School Library Pathfinder

Pathfinders are guides which are intended to help you get started doing research on a particular topic, both online and at your library. Although these resources are useful as a starting point for your research, they are not the only resources that are available to you.

Definition/Introduction

- *What is the topic? What does it cover?*

  Mythology is a collection of traditional stories that express the beliefs or values of a group of people. The stories often focus on human qualities such as good and evil.

- *Catalog Subject Headings or Keywords*

  Mythology
  > *See also specific national or ethnic group, e.g. Celtic mythology.*

- *Dewey Numbers*

  201 Religious mythology (formerly 291)
  398.2 Folk literature

Print Resources

- *Reference titles [dictionaries, encyclopedias, atlases, specific subject references]*

  Jordan, Michael. *Dictionary of Gods and Goddesses.* Facts On File, c2004.

  Mercatante, Anthony S. *The Facts On File Encyclopedia of World Mythology and Legend.* Facts On File, c2004.

  Mythology A to Z. Facts On File, c2004, c2000.

  Myths and Legends of the World. Macmillan Reference USA, c2000.

  Zimmerman, John Edward. *Dictionary of Classical Mythology.* Bantam, c1971, c1964.

- *General titles [nonfiction, any suitable fiction]*

  Be sure to check the library online catalog to find additional suitable materials.

  Hamilton, Virginia. *In the Beginning: Creation Stories From Around the World.* Harcourt Brace Jovanovich, c1988.

  January, Brendan. *The New York Public Library Amazing Mythology: A Book of Answers for Kids.* John Wiley, c2000.

  Mass, Wendy. *Gods and Goddesses.* Lucent Books, c2002.

Muten, Burleigh. *The Lady of Ten Thousand Names: Goddess Stories From Many Cultures.* Barefoot Books, c2001.

Steig, Jeanne. *A Gift From Zeus: Sixteen Favorite Myths.* Joanna Cotler Books, c2001.

■ *Journals*

Be sure to check any online periodical database at your school library for more.

"Creation Myth of the Hero Twins". *National Geographic*, Nov2004, Vol. 206 Issue 5, p48, 3p, 3c

Dignan, Jennifer. "The Myth of Medusa". *Storyworks*, Feb/Mar2004, Vol. 11 Issue 5, p26, 6p, 3c

"My Favorite Norse Myths". *Faces*, Jan2005, Vol. 21 Issue 5, p46, 1/5p

Skjærvø, P. Oktor. "Good vs. Evil". *Calliope*, Jan2005, Vol. 15 Issue 5, p8, 2p, 1c

Yellin, Janice. "Loved By the Gods". *Calliope*, Oct2003, Vol. 14 Issue 2, p27, 3p, 3c

Web Resources

Bulfinch's Mythology
http://www.bulfinch.org/
Classical collection of myths.

Encyclopedia Mythica
http://www.pantheon.org/
Encyclopedia of mythology, folklore, and religion.

Mything Links
http://www.mythinglinks.org/ct~creation.html
Creation myths and sacred narratives of creation.

Mythology
http://www.windows.ucar.edu/cgi-bin/tour_def/mythology/mythology.html
"Find out about the gods and goddesses of different cultures around the world, and the works of art people have created to give them expression."

Myths & Legends
http://home.comcast.net/~chris.s/myth.html
"Aside from the General section, these links are organized by region and language group, with those groups which produced written accounts of their myths and legends earlier, generally appearing closer to the beginning."

Mythweb
http://www.mythweb.com/
This site is devoted to the heroes, gods, and monsters of Greek mythology.

Topic: Poetry

Definition/Introduction

- ### *What is the topic? What does it cover?*

  In this pathfinder, you will study poetry to be able to appreciate the genre and to write your own poetry.

- ### *Catalog Subject Headings or Keywords*

  Poems
  Poetry
  > *See also the names of individual poets, (e.g. Dickinson, Emily; Frost, Robert) and styles of poetry.*

- ### *Dewey Numbers*

  808.81 general works
  811   American poetry
  821   British poetry

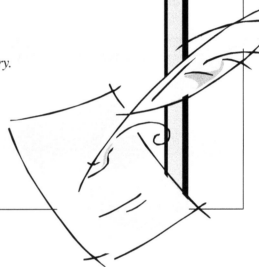

Print Resources

- ### *Reference titles [dictionaries, encyclopedias, atlases, specific subject references]*

  The Columbia Granger's Index to Poetry in Collected and Selected Works. Columbia University Press, c2004.

  The Facts On File Companion to 20th-Century Poetry. Facts On File, c2005.

  Notable Poets. Salem Press, c1998.

  Young, Sue. *The Scholastic Rhyming Dictionary.* Scholastic, c1994.

- ### *General titles [nonfiction, any suitable fiction]*

  Be sure to check the library online catalog to find additional suitable materials.

  Classic Poetry: An Illustrated Collection. Candlewick Press, c1998.

  The Everyman Anthology of Poetry For Children. Everyman's Library, c1994.

  Fletcher, Ralph J. *Poetry Matters: Writing a Poem From the Inside Out.* HarperCollins, c2002.

  Janeczko, Paul B. *How to Write Poetry.* Scholastic Reference, c2001, c1999.

  The Oxford Book of Children's Verse in America. Oxford University Press, c1985.

Language

- ## *Journals*

  Be sure to check any online periodical database at your school library for more.

  Kuebler, Sharon. "If You Like Fun Times, Write Rhymes". *Fun For Kidz*, Nov/Dec2004, Vol. 3 Issue 6, p14, 3p, 2c, 1bw

  "Make Your Own Haiku". *Kids Discover*, Nov2004, Vol. 14 Issue 11, p18, 1/2p

Web Resources

Craft of Poetry

http://www.uni.edu/~gotera/CraftOfPoetry/quatrain.html

A glossary and description of poetic types and elements are clearly written at this site from the University of Northern Iowa.

Poetry.com

http://www.poetry.com/

Site features over 5.1 million poets.

Poets.org

http://www.poets.org

Links to poetry and information about poets.

RhymeZone

http://www.rhymezone.com/

A search engine for rhyming words. Definitions, synonyms, and homophones are also given.

Shadow Poetry

http://www.shadowpoetry.com/

This site defines and gives you examples of several different types of poetry.

World Poetry Directory

http://www.unesco.org/poetry/bienvenue.php?initia=english

This Web site from the United Nations Educational, Scientific and Cultural Organization (UNESCO) has worldwide lists of poetry festivals, prizes, journals, and associations.

Topic: World Languages and Cultures

Definition/Introduction

■ *What is the topic? What does it cover?*

The use of language is the universal method of communication. Humans use language to connect to one another and to help understand one another. There are many languages spoken around the world. By studying a language other than your own, you will be able to communicate with more people. It will also help you understand your own language better.

■ *Catalog Subject Headings or Keywords*

World language
Foreign language
Language and languages
See also individual languages.

■ *Dewey Numbers*

400 Language – Be sure to browse the entire 400s.

Middle School Library Pathfinder

Pathfinders are guides which are intended to help you get started doing research on a particular topic, both online and at your library. Although these resources are useful as a starting point for your research, they are not the only resources that are available to you.

Print Resources

■ *Reference titles [dictionaries, encyclopedias, atlases, specific subject references]*

CultureGrams, 2005. ProQuest Information and Learning Co., c2004.

The Hutchinson Guide to the World. Oryx Press, c1998.

Worldmark Encyclopedia of Cultures and Daily Life. Gale, c1998.

See also language dictionaries for specific languages.

■ Journals

Be sure to check any online periodical database at your school library for more.

"Language. News for You", 10/27/93, Vol. 41 Issue 42, Language p4, 1/3p

"Languages Spoken by at Least 2 Million People". *World Almanac & Book of Facts*, 2004, p626, 2p, 1 chart

Web Resources

World Culture Sites:

Library of Congress Country Studies
http://lcweb2.loc.gov/frd/cs/cshome.html
Get a description and analysis of the historical setting and the social, economic, political, and national security systems and institutions of countries throughout the world.

Portals to the World
http://www.loc.gov/rr/international/portals.html
Links to electronic resources from around the world.

World Factbook
http://www.odci.gov/cia/publications/factbook/
Prepared by the Central Intelligence Agency. Lots of information about the countries of the world.

General Language Sites:

Babelfish Translator
http://babelfish.altavista.com/translate.dyn
Get a quick translation of a world language word or phrase at this site.

Say Hello to the World
http://www.ipl.org/youth/hello/
Internet Public Library designed this site that explores many world languages.

Word Reference.com
htttp://wordreference.com/
Quickly translate words into and from Spanish, Italian, and French.

Spanish:
The American Heritage Spanish Dictionary
http://education.yahoo.com/reference/dict_en_es/

French:
English to French, French to English Dictionary
http://www.freedict.com/onldict/fre.html

German:
German to English, English to German Dictionary
http://www.quickdic.de/index_e.html

Italian:
English to Italian, Italian to English Dictionary
http://www.freedict.com/onldict/ita.html

Latin:
English to Latin, Latin to English Dictionary
http://www.freedict.com/onldict/lat.html

Topic: Drug Abuse

Middle School Library Pathfinder

Pathfinders are guides which are intended to help you get started doing research on a particular topic, both online and at your library. Although these resources are useful as a starting point for your research, they are not the only resources that are available to you.

Definition/Introduction

- ### *What is the topic? What does it cover?*

    Drug abuse includes the abuse of narcotic and hallucinogenic substances and stimulants.

- ### *Catalog Subject Headings or Keywords*

    Drug abuse
    Addiction
    Narcotic habit
    Substance abuse
    Drug misuse
    See also specific names of drugs.

- ### *Dewey Numbers*

    362.29 Substance abuse (social welfare)
    613.8 Drug abuse (personal health)
    616.86 Drug abuse (diseases)

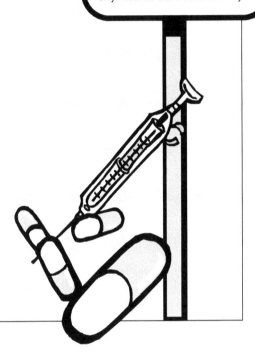

Print Resources

- ### *Reference titles [dictionaries, encyclopedias, atlases, specific subject references]*

    Drugs, Alcohol, and Tobacco: Learning About Addictive Behavior. Macmillan Reference USA, Thomson/Gale, c2003.

    Drugs and Controlled Substances: Information for Students. Gale, Thomson/Gale, c2003.

    Encyclopedia of Drugs, Alcohol, & Addictive Behavior. Macmillan Reference USA, c2001.

- ### *General titles [nonfiction, any suitable fiction]*

    Be sure to check the library online catalog to find additional suitable materials.

    Aretha, David. *Cocaine and Crack.* MyReportLinks.com Books, c2005.

    Aretha, David. *Steroids and Other Performance-Enhancing Drugs.* MyReportLinks.com Books, c2005.

    Aronson, Virginia. *How to Say No.* Chelsea House, c2000.

    Balcavage, Dynise. *Steroids.* Chelsea House, c2000.

    Clayton, Lawrence. *Amphetamines and Other Stimulants.* Rosen Pub. Group, 2001.

    Cobb, Allan B. *Heroin and Your Veins: The Incredibly Disgusting Story.* Rosen Central, 2000.

    Gottfried, Ted. *The Facts about Marijuana.* Benchmark Books, c2005.

    Lennard-Brown, Sarah. *Marijuana.* Raintree, c2005.

■ *Journals*

Be sure to check any online periodical database at your school library for more.

"Drug Addiction Is a Disease". *Scholastic Action*, 2/7/2005 Supplement, p5, 2p

Frank, Steven; Jones, Deborah. "Fighting Heroin with Heroin". *Time*, 2/14/2005, Vol. 165 Issue 7, p14, 1/3p, 1c

"Getting Help". *Current Health 2*, Mar2005, Vol. 31 Issue 7, p13, 1p, 1bw

Leinwand, Donna "Survey: More Teens Using OxyContin" *USA Today*, 12/22/2004

Web Resources

American Council for Drug Education
http://www.acde.org/youth/Research.htm
New facts sheets containing information about commonly abused drugs.

Life Bytes
http://www.lifebytes.gov.uk/drugs/drugs_menu.html
An appealing and fun site that is also informative. Includes sections on drug facts, risks, emergencies, and a quiz.

National Institute on Drug Abuse
http://www.nida.nih.gov/ResearchReports/ResearchIndex.html
This series of reports simplifies the science of research findings for the educated lay public, legislators, educational groups, and practitioners. The series reports on research findings of national interest.

National Institute on Drug Abuse: Mind Over Matter
http://www.drugabuse.gov/MOM/MOMIndex.html
A series of "stories" narrated by Sara Bellum about the brain's response to different drugs.

Topic: Genetic Diseases

Definition/Introduction

- ### *What is the topic? What does it cover?*

  Genetic diseases are disorders caused, at least in part, by defective genes or chromosomes.

- ### *Catalog Subject Headings or Keywords*

  Diseases
  Genetic disorders
  Genetic engineering
  Genetics
  Medical genetics

- ### *Dewey Numbers*

  362.1 Physical illness
  576.5 Genetics
  615.895 Specific therapies
  616 Diseases

Print Resources

- ### *Reference titles [dictionaries, encyclopedias, atlases, specific subject references]*

  Genetics. Macmillan Reference USA, Thomson/Gale, c2003.

  The Handbook of Genetic Communicative Disorders. Academic Press, c2001.

  Wynbrandt, James. *The Encyclopedia of Genetic Disorders and Birth Defects*. Facts On File, c2000.

- ### *General titles [nonfiction, any suitable fiction]*

  Be sure to check the library online catalog to find additional suitable materials.

  Fridell, Ron. *Decoding Life: Unraveling the Mysteries of the Genome*. Lerner Publications, c2005.

  Jacobs, Marian B. *Coping with Hereditary Diseases*. Rosen, c1999.

  Kupperberg, Paul. *How Do We Know the Nature of Disease*. Rosen, c2005.

  Yount, Lisa. *Gene Therapy*. Lucent Books, c2002.

- ### *Journals*

  Be sure to check any online periodical database at your school library for more.

  Berg, Kare. "Ethical Aspects of Early Diagnosis of Genetic Diseases". (cover story) World Health, Sep/Oct96, Vol. 49 Issue 5, p20, 2p, 2bw

Ebersole, Rene S. "Mending Genes". *Current Science,* 1/19/2001, Vol. 86 Issue 10, p4, 3p, 3c

Relos, Mariana. "What Are Genetic Diseases?" *Current Health 1*, Jan2003, Vol. 26 Issue 5, p29, 3p

Springen, Karen. "Using Genes as Medicine". (cover story) *Newsweek*, 12/6/2004, Vol. 144 Issue 23, p55, 2/3p, 1c

"What Are Genetic Diseases?" *Current Health 1*, Jan2003, Vol. 26 Issue 5, Special Section p4, 1/2p

Web Resources

Genetic and Rare Conditions Site
http://www.kumc.edu/gec/support/
Links to information about many genetic disorders.

Genetic Disease Information – Pronto!
http://www.ornl.gov/sci/techresources/Human_Genome/medicine/assist.shtml
Information from the Human Genome Project.

Genetic Disorder Corner
http://gslc.genetics.utah.edu/units/disorders/whataregd/
Information from the University of Utah about genetic disorders.

Genetics Home Reference
http://ghr.nlm.nih.gov/
The National Library of Medicine's Web site for consumer information about genetic conditions and the genes responsible for those conditions.

Your Genes, Your Health
http://www.ygyh.org/
A multimedia guide to genetic disorders.

Topic: Smoking and Tobacco

Definition/Introduction

- *What is the topic? What does it cover?*

  This topic includes information about smoking and the use of smokeless tobacco.

- *Catalog Subject Headings or Keywords*

  Smoking
  Tobacco
  Cigarettes
  Smokeless tobacco
  Lung cancer
  Secondhand smoke

- *Dewey Numbers*

  362.29 Social implications of tobacco addiction
  613.85 Physical aspects of tobacco addiction

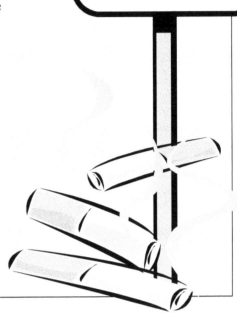

Print Resources

- *Reference titles [dictionaries, encyclopedias, atlases, specific subject references]*

  Health On File. Facts On File, c2002.

  Hirschfelder, Arlene B. *Encyclopedia of Smoking and Tobacco.* Oryx Press, c1999.

  Pampel, Fred C. *Tobacco Industry and Smoking.* Facts On File, c2004.

- *General titles [nonfiction, any suitable fiction]*

  Be sure to check the library online catalog to find additional suitable materials.

  Hirschfelder, Arlene B. *Kick Butts!: A Kid's Action Guide to a Tobacco-Free America.* Scarecrow Press, c2001.

  Landau, Elaine. *Cigarettes.* Franklin Watts, c2003.

  MacDonald, Joan Vos. *Tobacco and Nicotine Drug Dangers.* Enslow Publishers, c2000.

  Rackley, Jenny. *Nicotine.* Lucent Books, Thomson/Gale, c2002.

▪ *Journals*

Be sure to check any online periodical database at your school library for more.

"Cigs Can Kill". *Junior Scholastic*, 11/15/99, Vol. 102 Issue 7, p4, 1/3p

"Dangers of Secondhand Smoke". *Current Health 1*, Nov98, Vol. 22 Issue 3, p14, 3p, 1c

"5 Lies About Smoking". *Scholastic Choices*, Feb2002, Vol. 17 Issue 5, p13, 2/3p

"Smoking Slows Healing". *Current Health 2*, Mar2005, Vol. 31 Issue 7, p5, 1/2p, 1bw

Web Resources

Adolescent Smoking Statistics
http://www.lungusa.org/site/pp.asp?c=dvLUK9O0E&b=39868
Statistics and fact sheets regarding teen smoking.

Centers for Disease Control and Prevention
http://www.cdc.gov/doc.do/id/0900f3ec802346d8
Links to health topics regarding tobacco.

Secondhand Smoke: Protect Yourself From The Dangers
http://www.mayoclinic.com/invoke.cfm?objectid=055661AE-8008-40C8-A8526ED085B5CCC1
Tips for protecting yourself from the harm done by secondhand smoke.

Smokeless Tobacco: Addictive and Harmful
http://www.mayoclinic.com/invoke.cfm?objectid=BDFA0D03-F8D7-42B2-A8D23038227F0F3A
Information from the Mayo Clinic about the effects of smokeless tobacco.

Smoking Stinks!
http://kidshealth.org/kid/watch/house/smoking.html
All about the dangers of smoking.

Taking Action Against Secondhand Smoke
http://www.cdc.gov/tobacco/ETS_Toolkit/index.htm
What you need to know about secondhand smoke.

Teens and Tobacco Quiz: What Do You Know?
http://www.mayoclinic.com/invoke.cfm?objectid=7597CA6E-A0D6-4D3B-95968A1052792C76
Think you know all about tobacco and smoking? Take this quiz and see how much you really know.

Topic: Composers

Definition/Introduction

- ### *What is the topic? What does it cover?*

  A composer is the person who writes the music and/or words to a song.

- ### *Catalog Subject Headings or Keywords*

  Composers
  Song writers
  Musicians
  > *See also names of individual composers and styles of music.*

- ### *Dewey Numbers*

  780.92 Persons associated with music

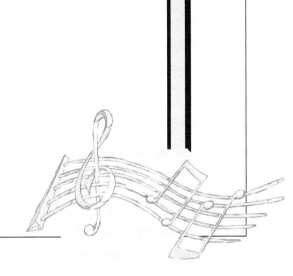

Print Resources

- ### *Reference titles [dictionaries, encyclopedias, atlases, specific subject references]*

  Baker's Student Encyclopedia of Music. Schirmer Books, c1999.

  Ewen, David. *American Songwriters: An H.W. Wilson Biographical Dictionary.* H.W. Wilson, c1987.

  Kennedy, Michael. *The Concise Oxford Dictionary of Music.* Oxford University Press, c2004.

  The Oxford Companion to Music. Oxford University Press, c2002.

  Slonimsky, Nicolas. *The Great Composers and Their Works.* Schirmer Books, c2000.

  World Musicians. H.W. Wilson Co., c1999.

- ### *General titles [nonfiction, any suitable fiction]*

  Be sure to check the library online catalog to find additional suitable materials.

  Brasch, Nicolas. *Classical and Opera.* Smart Apple Media, c2005, c2003.

  Bredeson, Carmen. *Ten Great American Composers.* Enslow Publishers, c2002.

  Geras, Adele. *The Random House Book of Opera Stories.* Random House, c1998, c1997.

  Hardy, P. Stephen. *Extraordinary People of the Harlem Renaissance.* Children's Press, c2000.

  Kallen, Stuart A. *Great Composers.* Lucent Books, 2000.

  Kallen, Stuart A. *The History of Classical Music.* Lucent Books, Thompson/Gale, c2003.

Krull, Kathleen. *Lives of the Musicians: Good Times, Bad Times (and What the Neighbors Thought)*. Harcourt, c2002, c1993.

Vernon, Roland. *Introducing Composers*. Chelsea House, c2001.

■ *Journals*

Be sure to check any online periodical database at your school library for more.

Hobson, Katherine. "Oops, Bach did it again". *U.S. News & World Report*, 4/8/2002, Vol. 132 Issue 11, p58, 1/4p, 1c

Satterfield, George D. "Mozart's Vienna". *Calliope*, Apr2003, Vol. 13 Issue 8, p18, 4p, 3c

Web Resources

Classical Net Composer Information sites
http://www.classical.net/music/links/complink.html
Provides links to composer information at Classical Net and on the Web.

Dallas Symphony Orchestra Kids Page
http://www.dsokids.com/2001/composerperiods.htm
Links to composers from the Renaissance to the present.

Essentials of Music
http://www.essentialsofmusic.com/
This site includes basic information about classical music. Brief biographies of nearly 70 composers are included as is a glossary of musical terms.

New York Philharmonic Kidzone!
http://www.nyphilkids.org/main.phtml
Information about composers as well as instruments and even some games to play!

Topic: Folk Music

Definition/Introduction

- ### *What is the topic? What does it cover?*

  Folk music originates among the common people of a nation or region and is spread about or passed down orally, often with considerable variation. It is also considered one genre of contemporary music in the style of traditional folk music.

- ### *Catalog Subject Headings or Keywords*

  Folk music
  Folk songs
  Blues music
  Country music
  Ballads
  > *See also folk tales and names of individual performers.*

- ### *Dewey Numbers*

  781.62 Folk music

Print Resources

- ### *Reference titles [dictionaries, encyclopedias, atlases, specific subject references]*

  Ammer, Christine. *The Facts on File Dictionary of Music*. Facts On File, c2004.

  Kennedy, Michael. *The Concise Oxford Dictionary of Music*. Oxford University Press, c2004.

  The Kingfisher Young People's Book of Music. Kingfisher, c1999, c1996.

  The Oxford Companion to Music. Oxford University Press, c2002.

  Slonimsky, Nicolas. *Baker's Dictionary of Music*. Schirmer Books, Prentice Hall International, c1997.

- ### *General titles [nonfiction, any suitable fiction]*

  Be sure to check the library online catalog to find additional suitable materials.
  American Musical Traditions. Schirmer Reference, Gale Group/Thomson Learning, c2002.
  The American Songbag. Harcourt Brace, c1990.
  Brasch, Nicolas. *Folk, Country, and Reggae*. Smart Apple Media, c2005, c2003.
  McNeil, Keith. *Moving West Songbook: With Historical Commentary*. WEM Records, c2003.
  Neimark, Anne E. *There Ain't Nobody That Can Sing Like Me: The Life of Woody Guthrie*. Atheneum Books for Young Readers, c2002.

Our Singing Country: Folk Songs and Ballads. Dover Publications, c2000.

Partridge, Elizabeth. *This Land Was Made For You and Me: The Life & Songs of Woody Guthrie.* Viking, c2002.

Shelton, Robert. *No Direction Home: The Life and Music of Bob Dylan.* Da Capo Press, c2003, c1986.

Sieling, Peter. *Folk Music.* Mason Crest Publishers, c2003.

■ Journals

Be sure to check any online periodical database at your school library for more.

There are many articles about individual artists.

Web Resources

Biographies of Folksingers
http://www.42explore.com/folkmusic2.htm
Links to biographies of a select group of folk music performers.

Folk Music
http://www.42explore.com/folkmusic.htm
Basics of folk music and lots of links to relevant sites.

Our Favorite Folk Songs
http://guitar-primer.com/Folk
Selection of folk music. Includes lyrics and music.

Popular Songs in American History
http://www.contemplator.com/america/
Tunes, lyrics, information, historical background, and tune related links.

Topic: Swing Era Music

Definition/Introduction

- ### *What is the topic? What does it cover?*

  In the 1930s, a new form of jazz had emerged, called "swing." Swing music was characterized by very large bands, fixed, usually written arrangements, and solos by individual musicians in turn instead of group improvisation. Swing bands typically used an upright or double bass instead of the tuba, which had often characterized Dixieland, and played repeated "riffs" to give the music its propulsive rhythmic force.

- ### *Catalog Subject Headings or Keywords*

  Jazz music
  Music
  Musicians
  > *See also names of individual performers, e.g. Ellington, Duke, 1899-1974.*

- ### *Dewey Numbers*

  780.92 Persons associated with music
  781.65 Jazz
  782.421/65 General principles of songs

Print Resources

- ### *Reference titles [dictionaries, encyclopedias, atlases, specific subject references]*

  Gusikoff, Lynn. *Guide to Musical America*. Facts On File, c1984.

  Penguin Encyclopedia of Popular Music. Penguin Books, c1998.

  Yanow, Scott. *Swing*. Miller Freeman Books, c2000.

- ### *General titles [nonfiction, any suitable fiction]*

  Be sure to check the library online catalog to find additional suitable materials. In addition to general music titles, search for biographies of notable people of the era.

  Albert, Richard N. *From Blues to Bop*. Anchor Books, c1992.

  Blackwood, Alan. *Music*. Steck-Vaughn Library, c1990.

  Oliphant, Dave. *The Early Swing Era, 1930 to 1941*. Greenwood Press, c2002.

■ *Journals*

Be sure to check the online periodical database, which lists a great many articles about "swing music."

Blumenthal, Bob. "First-person Memories of Swing". *Downbeat*, Jul 94, Vol. 61, Issue 7, p18

Chidley, Joe. "Sing, dance—and Be Worried". (cover story). *Maclean's*, 4/3/95, Vol. 108 Issue 14, p47

Loomis, Kiku. "Born in a Ballroom". *Dance Spirit*, Jan 2002, Vol. 6, Issue 1, p130

"Louis Armstrong". *Arts & Entertainment: Musicians & Composers*, 2002, p11

Singer, Barnett. "How Did Benny Goodman Get to Carnegie Hall". *American History*, Apr2001, Vol. 36 Issue 1, p22

Web Resources

Between the Wars
http://chnm.gmu.edu/courses/hist409/swing.html
How much do you know about the origins of swing music? Tap your knowledge and read about the history of swing.

Hypermusic History of Jazz
http://www.hypermusic.ca/jazz/mainmenu.html
An overview of the history of jazz including the changing and melding to create different forms from rag time to big band swing.

Swing Era
http://swingera.net/
As you browse the background articles and jukebox pages on The Swing Era, you'll soon discover there are quite a few bands, vocalists, and songs here.

Swing Era Introduction
http://xroads.virginia.edu/~ASI/musi212/emily/emain.html
An overview of the swing era with links to songs, musicians, history, and films.

Topic: Artists

Middle School Library Pathfinder

Pathfinders are guides which are intended to help you get started doing research on a particular topic, both online and at your library. Although these resources are useful as a starting point for your research, they are not the only resources that are available to you.

Definition/Introduction

- ### *What is the topic? What does it cover?*

  The study of art would not be complete without the study of the men and women who create the art. By learning about their lives, their influences, and their beliefs, it helps us to better understand their work.

- ### *Catalog Subject Headings or Keywords*

  Artists
  > *See also names of individual artists or style of art.*

- ### *Dewey Numbers*

  709.2 Persons in the arts

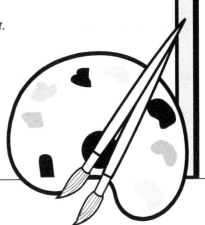

Print Resources

- ### *Reference titles [dictionaries, encyclopedias, atlases, specific subject references]*

  Encyclopedia of Artists. Oxford University Press, c2000.

  Greenway, Shirley. *Art: An A-Z Guide.* Franklin Watts, c2000.

  Kort, Carol. *A to Z of American Women in the Visual Arts.* Facts On File, c2002.

- ### *General titles [nonfiction, any suitable fiction]*

  Be sure to check the library online catalog to find additional suitable materials.

  Bolden, Tonya. *Wake Up Our Souls: A Celebration of Black American Artists.* Abrams, Published in association with the Smithsonian American Art Museum, c2004.

  Bolton, Linda. *Impressionism.* P. Bedrick Books, c2000.

  Cohen, Joel H. *Norman Rockwell: America's Best-Loved Illustrator.* Franklin Watts, c1997.

  Cole, Alison. *Renaissance.* DK Publishing, c2000.

  Hunter, Shaun. *Visual & Performing Artists.* Crabtree, c1999.

  McLanathan, Richard B.K. *Leonardo da Vinci.* Abrams, c1990.

  Talking With Artists: Conversations with Victoria Chess, Pat Cummings, Leo and Diane Dillon, Richard Egielski, Lois Ehlert, Lisa Campbell Ernst, Tom Feelings, Steven Kellogg, Jerry Pinkney, Amy Schwartz, Lane Smith, Chris Van Allsburg, and David Wiesner. Bradbury/Macmillan, c1992.

- ## *Journals*

    Be sure to check any online periodical database at your school library for more.

    Search the online periodical database by name of the artist or by particular artistic style.

Web Resources

Artists.org
http://www.the-artists.org/
Major modern and contemporary visual artists.

Famous Artists
http://www.k12.hi.us/~kapunaha/student_projects/famous_artists/famous_artists.htm
Savor the fruits of this student research project about famous Renaissance and Impressionist artists.

The Web Gallery of Art
http://www.kfki.hu/~arthp/welcome.html
The Web Gallery of Art contains more than 7,300 digital reproductions of European paintings and sculptures created between the years 1150-1750.

WWW Virtual Library: Museums Around the World
http://www.icom.org/vlmp/world.html
This site is a collection of World Wide Web services connected with museums around the world.

Technology Education

Topic: Bridges

Middle School Library Pathfinder

Pathfinders are guides which are intended to help you get started doing research on a particular topic, both online and at your library. Although these resources are useful as a starting point for your research, they are not the only resources that are available to you.

Definition/Introduction

- *What is the topic? What does it cover?*

  This pathfinder deals with the construction and science involved in building bridges.

- *Catalog Subject Headings or Keywords*

  Bridges
  See also names of specific bridges and styles of bridges.

- *Dewey Numbers*

  624.2 Civil engineering – Bridges
  725 Architecture of public structures

Print Resources

- *Reference titles [dictionaries, encyclopedias, atlases, specific subject references]*

  Horobin, Wendy. *How It Works: Science and Technology*, 3rd ed. Marshall Cavendish, c2003.

  How In The World? Reader's Digest Association, c1990.

  The New Book of Popular Science. Grolier, c1990.

  The Raintree Illustrated Science Encyclopedia. Raintree, c1991.

  Science and Technology Illustrated: The World Around Us. Encyclopaedia Britannica, c1984.

- *General titles [nonfiction, any suitable fiction]*

  Be sure to check the library online catalog to find additional suitable materials.

  Dunn, Andrew. *Bridges*. Thomson Learning, c1993.

  Macaulay, David. *Building Big*. Houghton Mifflin, c2000.

  Olney, Ross Robert. *They Said It Couldn't Be Done*. Dutton, c1979.

■ *Journals*

Be sure to check any online periodical database at your school library for more.

"The Art of Arch-ery". *Kids Discover*, Jun2004, Vol. 14 Issue 6, p6, 2p, 6c

Normile, Dennis; Vizard, Frank. "A bridge so far". (cover story) *Popular Science*, Mar98, Vol. 252 Issue 3, p48, 6p, 7 diagrams, 2 maps, 6c

"Portable Battle Bridge". *Odyssey*, Nov2001, Vol. 10 Issue 8, p36, 1p, 1 diagram, 1c

Soard, Lori. "Confederation Bridge". *Faces*, Nov99, Vol. 16 Issue 3, p30, 4p, 2c

Web Resources

Building a Suspension Bridge
http://www.salvadori.org/aobc/
Step by step instructions for building a model suspension bridge.

Building Big – Bridges
http://www.pbs.org/wgbh/buildingbig/bridge/
Explore large structures and what it takes to build them with BUILDING BIG™, based on a five-part PBS television series from WGBH Boston.

Geometry of Bridge Construction
http://www.faculty.fairfield.edu/jmac/rs/bridges.htm
Explanations of the four kinds of bridges and some combinations.

How Bridges Work
http://travel.howstuffworks.com/bridge.htm
A look at the three major types of bridges so that you can understand how each one works. The type of bridge used depends on various features of the obstacle.

Topic: Career Exploration

Definition/Introduction

- ### *What is the topic? What does it cover?*

  It is never too early to be thinking about careers and exploring different ones. By being exposed to a multitude of opportunities, you can begin to narrow in on your desired career as an adult.

- ### *Catalog Subject Headings or Keywords*

  Careers
  Occupations
  Professions
  Vocational guidance
  See also specific careers.

- ### *Dewey Numbers*

  331.7 Labor by industry and occupation

Print Resources

- ### *Reference titles [dictionaries, encyclopedias, atlases, specific subject references]*

  Career Discovery Encyclopedia. Ferguson Pub., c2003.

  The Directory of Jobs and Careers Abroad. Vacation Work , c2002.

  Encyclopedia of Careers and Vocational Guidance. Ferguson Pub., c2003.

  Professional Careers Sourcebook: Where to Find Help Planning Careers that Require College or Technical Degrees. Thomson/Gale, c2002.

  The Top 100: The Fastest Growing Careers for the 21st Century. Ferguson Pub., c2001.

  VGM's Careers Encyclopedia. VGM Career Books, c2002.

- ### *General titles [nonfiction, any suitable fiction]*

  Be sure to check the library online catalog to find additional suitable materials.

  Heading Out: The Start of Some Splendid Careers. Bloomsbury Children's Books, Distributed to the trade by Holtzbrinck Publishers, c2003.

  Kiefer, Jeanne. *Jobs for Kids: A Smart Kid's Q & A Guide.* Millbrook Press, c2003.

  O'Donnell, Annie. *Computer Animator.* Rosen Central, c2000.

  Reeves, Diane Lindsey. *Career Ideas For Kids Who Like Money.* Facts On File, c2001.

  Reeves, Diane Lindsey. *Career Ideas For Kids Who Like Music and Dance.* Facts On File, c2001.

  Reeves, Diane Lindsey. *Career Ideas For Kids Who Like Travel.* Facts On File, c2001.

■ *Journals*

Be sure to check any online periodical database at your school library for more.

Chevat, Richie. "Where Do I Go With . . . Music?" *Career World*, Nov/Dec2004, Vol. 33 Issue 3, p26, 4p, 1 chart, 3c

Faiad, Andrea. "Adventure Careers". *Career World*, Jan2005, Vol. 33 Issue 4, p6, 4p, 5c

Lim, Paul J.; Mannix, Margaret; Smart, Tim. "Chewing Over Job Losses". *U.S. News & World Report*, 4/19/2004, Vol. 136 Issue 13, pEE16, 1/2p, 1c

"Which Job Is For You?" *Owl*, Nov 2004, Vol. 29 Issue 9, p9, 1/2p

Web Resources

Bureau of Labor Statistics Career Information
http://www.edina.k12.mn.us/valleyview/media/pathfinders/career.htm
Information about many careers. Includes employment projections.

Career Voyages
http://www.careervoyages.gov/
Explore career options and discover the high growth jobs with better wages and a brighter future.

Exploring Occupations
http://www.umanitoba.ca/counselling/careers.html
Information on almost 200 careers.

Mapping Your Future
http://www.mapping-your-future.org/MHSS/
"Welcome to the guided tour for middle and high school students. On this tour, you'll be able to find out more about planning for your future. You can leave the tour at any time to find out more about a subject by clicking on the highlighted text."

Occupational Outlook Handbook
http://www.bls.gov/oco/
"The *Occupational Outlook Handbook* is a nationally recognized source of career information, designed to provide valuable assistance to individuals making decisions about their future work lives."

U.S. Department of Labor
http://www.dol.gov/asp/fibre/main.htm
Information on finding a job. Find out about child labor laws.

Topic: Consumer Education

Definition/Introduction

■ *What is the topic? What does it cover?*

Everyone is a consumer at some time. The more you know, the more likely that you will be a smart consumer. Knowing about products, how to compare similar products and knowing the value of items contribute to being a good shopper. In this pathfinder, we will be looking at various sources of consumer education.

■ *Catalog Subject Headings or Keywords*

Consumer education
Consumers
Shopping

■ *Dewey Numbers*

381.3 Commercial policy
640.73 Evaluation and purchasing

Print Resources

■ *General titles [nonfiction, any suitable fiction]*

Be sure to check the library online catalog to find additional suitable materials.

Green, Mark J. *The Consumer Bible: 1001 Ways To Shop Smart.* Workman, c1998.

Menhard, Francha Roffe. *Teen Consumer Smarts: Shop, Save, and Steer Clear of Scams.* Enslow Publishers, c2002.

Satin, Morton. *Food Alert!: The Ultimate Sourcebook for Food Safety.* Facts On File, c1999.

Shelly, Susan. *The Complete Idiot's Guide to Money for Teens.* Alpha Books, c2001.

■ *Journals*

Be sure to check any online periodical database, at your school library for more.

Bryant Quinn, Jane. "Making the Right Call". *Newsweek*, 4/26/2004. Vol. 143 Issue 17, p40, 1/2p;

Chatzky, Jean. "Annual Consumer Complaint List". *Time*, 2/21/2005. Vol. 165 Issue 8, p65, 3/4p, 7c

Goldstein, Josh. "Hackers steal consumer info from security company." *Philadelphia Inquirer, The* (PA), 02/18/2005

"Gone Phishing". *Time*, 5/3/2004, Vol.163 Issue 18, p91, 1/8p

Stern, Linda. "Wanna Deal? Click Here". *Newsweek*, 3/22/2004, Vol. 143 Issue 12, p65, 2p, 1c

Web Resources

Consumer.gov
http://www.consumer.gov
Your resource for consumer information from the federal government.

Consumer Reports Online
http://www.consumerreports.org/main/home.jsp
"Consumer Reports® and ConsumerReports.org® are published by Consumers Union, an expert, independent nonprofit organization whose mission is to work for a fair, just, and safe marketplace for all consumers and to empower consumers to protect themselves. To achieve this mission, we test, inform, and protect."

Federal Citizen Information Center
http://www.pueblo.gsa.gov/
For years, consumers have written to Pueblo, Colorado 81009 for timely, practical information they trust. FCIC provides the answers to questions about the federal government and everyday consumer issues whether citizens write, call, or log on.

How Stuff Works
http://www.howstuffworks.com/
An excellent Web site that shows you how common, everyday objects work. Understanding will help you to become a better consumer.

Juvenile Products Manufacturers Association
http://www.jpma.org/
"This site is dedicated to promoting and informing consumers, the industry and our membership about the safe use of juvenile products, industry issues and the Juvenile Products Manufacturers Association."

Topic: Inventions and Inventors

Definition/Introduction

■ What is the topic? What does it cover?

Behind every new discovery is an inventor. An inventor is someone who can see how things work and how they can work better. They can see things that don't even exist and make them happen. When you log-on to the Internet or turn on the television, you probably don't wonder about who invented these items that we take for granted. In this unit, we will meet some of the people behind the great inventions.

■ Catalog Subject Headings or Keywords

Inventions
Inventors
Creation
Technology

■ Dewey Numbers

608 Inventions
609 Inventors

Print Resources

■ Reference titles [dictionaries, encyclopedias, atlases, specific subject references]

Eureka! UXL, c1995.

Famous First Facts: A Record of First Happenings, Discoveries, and Inventions in World History. H.W. Wilson, c2000.

Historical Inventions on File: Understanding Science By Re-Creating Key Inventions. Facts On File, c1994.

Langone, John. *The New How Things Work: Everyday Technology Explained.* National Geographic Society, c2004.

Popular Science: Science Year By Year: Discoveries and Inventions From the Last Century That Shape Our Lives. Scholastic Reference, c2001.

Sachs, Jessica Snyder. *The Encyclopedia of Inventions.* Franklin Watts, c2001.

World of Invention. Gale, c2001.

- ## *General titles [nonfiction, any suitable fiction]*

  Be sure to check the library online catalog to find additional suitable materials.

  Haskins, James. *Outward Dreams: Black Inventors and Their Inventions*. Walker, c2003.

  Hudson, Wade. *Scientists, Healers, and Inventors: An Introduction For Young Readers*. Just Us Books, c2003.

  Sullivan, Otha Richard. *African American Inventors*. John Wiley, c1998.

  Tomecek, Steve. *What a Great Idea!: Inventions That Changed the World*. Scholastic Nonfiction, c2003.

  Vare, Ethlie Ann. *Women Inventors and Their Discoveries*. Oliver Press, c1993.

  Life & Times in 20th-Century America. Greenwood Press, c2004.

- ## *Journals*

  Be sure to check any online periodical database at your school library for more.

  "The Coolest Inventions of 2004". *Time for Kids*, 12/10/2004, Vol. 10 Issue 11, p4, 3p, 12c

  Fradin, Judy. "Off to a Good Start". *Cobblestone*, Jan2005, Vol. 26 Issue 1, p4, 4p, 6c

  Hopkins, Heather M. "International Inventions In The 1800s". *Cobblestone*, Jan2005, Vol. 26 Issue 1, p16, 2p

  "Who Did What?" *Kids Discover*, Feb2005, Vol. 16 Issue 2, p18, 1/3p

Web Resources

Famous Inventions and Inventors
http://www.bkfk.com/inventions/
Famous inventors and inventions from around the world.

National Inventors Hall of Fame
http://www.invent.org/hall_of_fame/1_0_0_hall_of_fame.asp
Each year, the Selection Committee of the National Inventors Hall of Fame Foundation selects inventors for induction.

Smithsonian Institution Inventors and Innovation
http://www.si.edu/resource/faq/nmah/invent.htm
Lots of information about inventions and inventors through the ages.

Zoom Inventors and Inventions
http://www.zoomwhales.com/inventors/
Timeline of inventions and alphabetical links to inventors.

Index

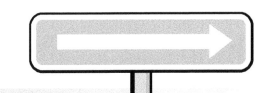

A

African American history 61
Alternative energy .71
American Revolution 29
Ancient Africa 7
Ancient China 9
Ancient Egypt 11
Ancient Greece 13
Ancient India 15
Ancient Rome 17
Animals 97
Artists 149
Astronomy 77

B

Biomes 99
Bridges 153

C

Career exploration 155
Chemical elements 73
Child labor 41
Civil rights movement 49
Civil War 37
Colonial America 27
Composers 141
Consumer education 159
Countries/travel 53

D

Drug abuse 133

E

Earthquakes 79
El Niño 81
Endangered species 101
Explorers 25

F

Folk music 143
Folklore/folktales 123
Food chain 103
Fractals 115

G

Genetic diseases .135
Great Depression .43

H

Hispanic American culture 63
Hurricanes 83

I

Immigration 55
Invasive species .105
Inventions/inventors 159

L

Landforms 85
Lewis and Clark .33
Light and optics .75

M

Martin Luther King, Jr. 51
Mathematicians .117
Middle Ages 21
Minerals 87
Mythology 125

N

Native Americans .57
Nutrition 107

O

Oceans 89

P

Poetry 127
Presidents 65

R

Rainforests 109
Renaissance 23
The Research Project 1

Index

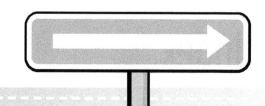

S

Science fair projects 111
Severe weather 91
Smoking and tobacco 137
Swing era music .145

T

Tessellations 119
Tornadoes 93

U

U.S. Constitution .31
Underground Railroad 35

V

Vikings 19
Volcanoes 95

W

Westward Expansion 39
Women's history .59
World languages/cultures 129
World religions 67
World War I 45
World War II 47

9 781586 832001